Routledge Revivals

Goethe

First published in 1972, *Goethe* presents a biography looking at one of the few great Europeans to be universally recognized as a hero of culture, and in the light of modern sociological thought puts the hero into his background, human, social and political. Goethe is seen in the context of his times- not as the Great Poet or the Great Lover but as the worried contemporary of the French Revolution and Napoleon. The author is much more interested than most biographers in the mature Goethe and the problems of the poet's old age. This stems from his intense preoccupation with Goethe's friend and biographer Eckermann, whose Conversations (for which Eckermann is ranked by many with Boswell) he is re-editing.

This is an interesting read for scholars of German language & literature and European literature.

Goethe

New Perspectives on a Writer and his Time

Derek Van Abbe

First published in 1972
by George Allen & Unwin Ltd.

This edition first published in 2024 by Routledge
4 Park Square, Milton Park, Abingdon, Oxon, OX14 4RN

and by Routledge
605 Third Avenue, New York, NY 10017

Routledge is an imprint of the Taylor & Francis Group, an informa business

Publisher's Note
The publisher has gone to great lengths to ensure the quality of this reprint but points out that some imperfections in the original copies may be apparent.

Disclaimer
The publisher has made every effort to trace copyright holders and welcomes correspondence from those they have been unable to contact.

A Library of Congress record exists under ISBN: 0048380024

ISBN: 978-1-032-82057-6 (hbk)
ISBN: 978-1-003-50339-2 (ebk)
ISBN: 978-1-032-82061-3 (pbk)

Book DOI 10.4324/9781003503392

GOETHE

New Perspectives on a Writer and his Time

Derek Van Abbé
M.A., Ph. D.
Head of Department of Languages
Polytechnic of the South Bank, London

London: George Allen and Unwin Ltd
Ruskin House Museum Street

ISBN 0 04 838001 6 hardback
0 04 838002 4 paper

Printed in Great Britain
in 11 point Baskerville type
by Clarke, Doble & Brendon Ltd
Plymouth

Preface

One main reason for the continued production of books on well-known subjects is the obvious need to rethink Knowledge for every generation. It is not only that research uncovers new facts; each new generation looks at the old facts from its own angle and feels dissatisfied with the interpretation placed on the old facts by the old interpreters. In much the same way each generation turns away from translations of the world's great literary works into the language of bygone ages.

Our generation is more interested in sociological links between life and the Arts than many other generations have been, especially those immediately preceding us. Whilst it would be too sweeping a generalization to say that 'we are all Marxists now', there can be no doubt that the work of great modern Marxist critics like Lukács, Mayer and Bloch permeates the thought of very many writers on the Arts who do not even know that they are near-Marxists, or who, like most English critics, have never read a line of any consciously Marxist theoretician. The work of Marcuse, Adorno, Benjamin and many others has also contributed to disseminating this interest in sociological links, whilst our age is now reaping the harvest of sub-Marxist theoreticians of a slightly earlier period, such as Edmund Wilson, Basil Willey, Levin Schücking and even, in some lights, the Leavises. There is also a move in this direction in German studies, although the tradition of militant aestheticism is still strongly represented: the work of Roy Pascal, Walter Bruford and Richard Samuel is still scarcely recognized as being an approach to our subject which is qualitatively different from studies in the world of artistic impressions.

The biography of Goethe which follows is an attempt to write a literary study of this modern kind. Goethe is seen not as a case-history for the psychoanalyst or a treasure-chest of poetic analysis, but as a poet living in contact with his day and reacting to it in ways now conventional, now personal. In order to set the scene for this study, it will be necessary to comment, from time to time, on the world in which the poet lived. We cannot fail to be interested in Goethe's approach to the kind of political world in which he lived and to that end we must also have at least a nodding acquaintance with the political atmosphere of that world, comparing it, as far as we can (as non-qualified historians and sociologists) with other political worlds with which we are acquainted.

It is well known that in the eighteenth century Germany (still the Holy Roman Empire, even though the Empire's government was barely recognized) was nothing like as advanced as England and France. England had already become a fairly centralized state with a thriving capital and was beginning to progress towards that Industrial Revolution which was to change completely the social climate of the nineteenth and twentieth centuries. Though the change was imminent its effects were at first felt only by those who were sensitive to the indications which could be read in the works of writers and of the journalists who were already beginning to make their appearance on the English scene. France was in the throes of a much less visible revolution for most of the century, though the turn to political violence from 1789 tended to focus attention on that violence and the changes it brought and to distract attention from the underlying ideological structures. As opposed to England and France, Germany was a large country made up of small autocratically-ruled states of varying sizes. Where London and Paris concentrated intellectuals into one centre, Germany had no major centre but only, and for shorter periods of time, minor centres favouring certain aspects of the general intellectual ferment of the age. If there was from the 1730s on a growing political and ideological awareness amongst the German intelligentsia (assuming at times a mania for Liberty dating from the 1760s), it is not a constant phenomenon which can be studied as a monolithic whole.

Politically it is probable that in most of the German states there was even more to complain about than there was for the intellectuals to complain about in France. But this dissenting thought and activity, which would, as in France, have reached a peak in the 1780s, was inhibited in Germany by the diffuse nature of political activity. In a smallish state the 'trouble-maker' was quickly identified and dealt with – as the cases of Weishaupt and Schubart show very dramatically. The resentful intellectual felt himself isolated and, in his loneliness, often sought consolation in Utopian fantasies. Thus, intimidated, lonely, and rudderless, the German writer failed to make the same impact on European thought of Voltaire, Rousseau, Diderot, Hume or Adam Smith.

There is, however, a further phenomenon which calls for more analysis than it has usually been given. From the time of the publication of *Werther* and *Götz von Berlichingen* German letters were dominated by the figure of Goethe, and, for all the qualities which the young genius possessed, it is a saddening reflection on the German situation that he was essentially a non-political thinker. He was indeed often attacked for this by contemporary rebels and called in round terms a 'Fürstenknecht' by the immature liberals and democrats of the immediate post-Napoleonic age. One hesitates to take up their criticisms again but it is a task which needs to be done, in order both to see whether there is any real truth in the allegations, and to discover, in any case, why this should have been so, or why Goethe should have got himself into this position *vis-à-vis* young men whose generous sympathies seem to us today not to have been entirely misplaced.

The phenomenon of Goethe's apolitical writing is all the more striking because his famous predecessors and contemporaries were very obviously political. Even the 'seraphic' Klopstock tended to the Left politically, to the point of dancing round a Tree of Liberty in 1789; his immediate disciples, the young writers of the Göttingen school, were deeply imbued with a sense of the need for an attack on privilege. In his highly personal fashion Hamann too was a savage critic of tyranny and he passed on his moral earnestness to Herder, who was often depressed by the unpolitical unwisdom (as he thought it) of his greater friend and protector in Weimar. There is deep intellectual disquiet in many of the writings of Lessing, and younger men steeped in this tradition – like Grimm, Forster and Klootz – were even led to throw in their lot with the French revolutionaries.

The first hint of ways in which this fermentation of liberal enthusiasm could be side-tracked is given by Wieland. The writers mentioned in the last paragraph were all serious-minded, essentially political and, wherever possible, activists. Wieland was an example of the gifted writer who is only public-spirited to the extent of using mass media as a platform for his own gratification: Wieland edited the most successful 'little magazine' of the century in Germany, but showed – by his very success, it may be said – that talk about politics can be used as a substitute for personal engagement in politics. In the same way Wieland's novels made use of the great themes of the day for artistic purposes without developing them in any sense likely to charge up the batteries of the discontented readers.

Goethe reacted in this same apolitical fashion from the very outset of his career. In the school of radical thinkers like Herder and Merck he might himself have become a political activist, but did not. It is most revealing, from this angle, that his immediate reaction to the galvanizing influence of Herder was to make a 'revolutionary' play out of the autobiography of a Renaissance robber-knight. There is never in his biography any hint that he might have thought in terms of a contemporary work focusing the excitement of the age as Lessing did in *Emilia Galotti* and as Schiller was to do in *Die Räuber*. *Faust* may well owe much to the impact on the young poet of a politically damaging criminal case which he attended as a novice lawyer; but the seriousness of the political implications of the theme of infanticide was entirely subsumed by Goethe's nature into one of the great love-stories of European literature. This same reaction was repeated in the biographical events which form the background to the genesis of *Werther*, the novel which gave Goethe European celebrity. What is, from the political standpoint, the most interesting feature of the success of *Werther*, is that it turned out to be one of those works which seem to arise in every revolutionary age, channelling generous enthusiasms which were just short of revolutionary boiling point: in this context we could say the same thing about the great tragedies of Shakespeare in the Elizabethan context, about *Le Cid* as a product of the days of the Parisian Fronde, about *Tom Jones* in the age of the 'Glorious Revolution', *Die Weber* in the age of the *Sozialistengesetze* and Anouilh's *Antigone* during the French resistance period.

But this is not all. The charge of 'Fürstenknecht' was levelled at Goethe above all because of his long connection with the court of Weimar. By accepting the invitation to Duke Karl August's court and staying there for the rest of his long life, Goethe finally turned his back on any possible revolutionary interpretation of German reality. As the 'Young Germans' were to hold, he can well be said to have bolstered up the court-system in Germany for its continued life up to 1918. It is difficult to see how Goethe could have done anything else, and this biography will chart the steps by which he inevitably came to tread this path – and what it cost him. But the fact that he did this was also to be responsible for the parallel retrogression of a potentially even more revolutionary spirit, that of Schiller. But the contrasting careers of Kleist, Büchner and Heine offer us little hope that any conceivable alternative development would have given the world as much as it gained from Goethe's decision to turn 'Fürstenknecht'.

As this biography will show, Goethe was always aware of his false position. His escape to Italy after only ten years in Weimar is an early acknowledgment of his malaise. The fact that he returned showed, moreover, conscious acceptance of the fact that a poet must choose between the garret and the leash. To cover up his servitude Goethe adopted the stiff 'Hofrat' manner about which later contemporaries were to complain: he could not afford to relax as less responsible individuals may. What is more interesting to critics, however, is the fact that he continued to try to bring his latent spirit of revolt into his later works. In this sense *Tasso* is indeed a 'reinforced' *Werther*, in which there is much more strain and much less attempt to strike 'beautiful' poses. The study of *Die natürliche Tochter* in this light is very rewarding, if possibly unfamiliar to those critics whose main interests are in aesthetics: much more should be done for this drama on the fruitful lines of Ursula Wertheim's parallel study of the political implications of the *Divan*. The despairing 'democratic' Utopianism of *Wilhelm Meisters Wanderjahre* is obscured by the monumental 'difficulty' of its style, which is a pity because its 'message' ought to have been welcomed by German democrats to a much greater degree than it has been. But it is still not possible to absolve Goethe from the charge that, being essentially an apolitical genius, he did not give his countrymen a clear lead in their fight against tyranny: when he gave his genius its head it produced great masterpieces which were essentially for the enjoyment of life and not for the conquest of frustration. Thus there is not much point in attempting too essentially political an interpretation of *Faust*, or *Iphigenie* or of *Wilhelm Meisters Lehrjahre*. In the sense of living a schizophrenic life between thought and reality Goethe is very German. It was unfortunate for the devoted Eckermann that so much of the wisdom of the mature Goethe was passed on to him only in a coded form which he was not capable of grasping – and, of course, it was cowardly of the great man to think of leaving *behind* him a record of what he really thought.

Long before his last decade Goethe had become an object of pilgrimage to young writers and thinkers. This happens to all great men who live long lives. One result of this European hero-worship is that we learn much more about the lives of such men than we normally do about those of our friends and neighbours. In the case of the biography of a great lyric poet we are particularly interested in the loves which stimulated his constant ability to write the kind of verses most men can only write at the stage of puberty. Hence the need to pry into Goethe's sex-life. Here too we can, of course, follow themes which have great political relevance: thus Goethe's decision to live openly with his mistress went far beyond what was normally expected of a good German 'Untertan'. But the poet paid for his rashness: the first decade of the nineteenth century was painful for him in more ways than one. Of all his flirtations, possibly that with the spirited Marianne von Willemer was the only one that may be said to have assisted his intellectual development; the others produced some good poetry but all undermined his physical constitution that little bit more. To add to his personal worries there was the strain of looking after his son and daughter-in-law, a development which, with his usual brilliant foresight, the poet had foreseen in *Götz von Berlichingen* when he talked of the way great men are responsible for casting the dark shadow which eclipses their children.

All great men offer posterity salutary lessons in lifemanship. But it is impossible to keep up with the passing of the generations. Goethe is no exception to this rule and much of the detail of his biography is simply a contribution to the disillusionment of eager young readers. It is hoped that this biography may have met some of the requirements of the revolutionary young with whom so much of it has been discussed. It is part of the curse of Adam that one generation's pace-maker merely becomes the next's 'Scheißliberaler'!

D.V.A.

Cambridge
October 1970

Contents

Chapter 1

Frankfurt am Main and the Eighteenth Century

Johann Wolfgang Goethe was born in the Imperial Free City of Frankfurt am Main in 1749. None of the implications of this simple statement can be taken for granted in assessing the 'influences' which were to mould his character. So let us examine them more closely.

A child born in 1749 would enter his teens around 1762. This is the real meaning of the process of giving a writer's date of birth: to find the time when influences from the outside world begin to exert their sway on his conscious mind. If he is capable of any development, this will be the time when he does change and grow. Thus it is not from the date of birth that one should reckon most profitably but from the time when the bright young writer begins to react consciously to the outside world. In Goethe's case we are told that this was very early. He was a precocious child; we have clumsy but pert verses written by him before 1762. It is significant that some of them are written in English and others in French. This is a measure of the backwardness of purely German culture during the middle years of the eighteenth century: a firmly German style had still not properly established itself. This is not to say that there had been no German culture before this period. What we see in the eighteenth century was largely a result of the shocking catastrophe of the seventeenth century, which gave the quietus to that wonderful flowering of the human spirit in Germany which, only a century before, had culminated in the work of writers like Hutten and Sachs, artists like Holbein and Dürer and, towering over all, Martin Luther.

Luther's achievement so dominated his century that the fine arts were all turned to the service of God, and the creative spirit was constrained to serve theology. Only at the end of the sixteenth century was there a revival of some kind of secular culture outside the Church; the considerable intellectual promise of the small aristocratic and upper middle-class circles which re-formed in Germany in the first two decades of the seventeenth century was even influential abroad (it is striking, for example, to find how many of those connected with the foundation in London in the mid-seventeenth century of the Royal Society were Germans, now refugees from their own war-torn land).[1]

Everything in Germany froze, in fact, in the grip of the Thirty Years War. The slaughter was terrible; it has been calculated that Germany lost in all a third of its population between 1618 and 1648. Cities were taken and re-taken; each of these military manœuvres meant, naturally, brutal and illiterate soldiers stealing, raping and pillaging. The result was to destroy what might be called the humus of social intercourse: Germany is a large country and, to function properly, it requires mobility between its provincial centres, so that fashions and ideas pass quickly between one and the next. Not only was travel almost at a standstill after 1648, but even within the cities people had got into the habit of avoiding their neighbours, not merely because gatherings were likely to be suspected of political or religious subversion, but also because of the risk of infection in a situation where plague was an everyday occurrence.

Perhaps as bad as any of the deleterious influences of the religious war, however, was the fact that during and after it the secular revival associated with the growth of the so-called 'language societies' was stunted, and the Arts once more harnessed in slavery to the chariot of theology. A society at war for thirty years needs propagandists, not poets. The marvel is not that the literature survived, but that some respectable literature was born out of the sufferings of the war (such as Grimmelshausen's extra-

[1] W. H. G. Armytage gives some idea of this influence in his rather summary and badly produced *The German Influence on English Education* (Routledge 1969). It is a field on which little good research has been done.

ordinary picaresque novel *Simplicissimus*, and the frequently remarkable lyric-cum-religious poetry of the unorthodox Jesuit Friedrich von Spee). Despite these exceptions the position of literature after the return of peace was bad. The German states were impoverished and education had suffered greatly from the uncertainty of the times. Not surprisingly, the development of the German language into a literary medium, a process which had begun with the rapid spread of Luther's translations of the Bible in the previous century, had been arrested; and the language itself had been bastardized to an almost incredible extent by decades of foreign occupation. German was adulterated with French, Italian, Spanish and even Slavic words, phrases and constructions. In the first half of the eighteenth century leading critics were still having to stand up and call loudly on their fellow-countrymen to try to set their linguistic house in order.[2]

Indeed it may be said that the whole of the second half of the seventeenth century was devoted simply to reviving the social life of Germany. Once this had been achieved the signals were set for progress, but this progress could only be slow whilst Germany, from the political viewpoint, was still the sport of the European political leaders. Now it is well known that the 'independence' of Germany was not achieved until the very middle of the eighteenth century, with the rule of Frederick II of Prussia. This does not imply that Frederick's success was totally unexpected or won simply through the brilliance of his own character: Frederick underlined, for the great powers of Europe, the fact that Germany was no longer simply a 'Tom Tiddler's ground' in which they could go fishing for practical (perhaps financial) advantage when no other parts of their foreign policy would work. Frederick's father and grandfather had been working at this solidification of their state before him; it was Frederick who had the panache to execute a series of brilliant acts of political piracy, the luck to carry them off successfully (despite strenuous resistance from the combined might of Russia, Austria and France), and the charisma of a king who really did think of himself as 'the first servant of his State', and who interfered (even though the success

[2] See the thorough and elegant *The Emergence of German as a Literary Language* by E. Blackall (Cambridge 1959).

of his interference cannot always be adjudged to have been either beneficent or lasting) in every facet of his country's social, economic – and literary – life.

In other parts of Germany the post-1648 recovery was equally marked, though not necessarily so spectacular. The essential aspect, for our purpose, is that by 1750 the after-effects of the Thirty Years War were at last beginning to be shaken off. From one viewpoint one may well marvel: did it really take so long for Germany to recover? From another aspect one should see how remarkable it is that it is precisely from this moment, in fact, from the 1750s, that German literature begins its rapid ascent to European rank. It took a century to overcome the effects of the religious wars, not least because of the freeze which theological control imposed on German minds (traces of this may *still* be descried). It was fortunate for the Germans that the winds which blew in this first half-century from England and France were those of the Enlightenment, a crusade which was essentially directed at demolishing the superstitions and teleologies of medieval relics in Western thought. One of the proofs of the slowness of German recovery is the great opposition that had to be overcome by such pioneers of modern thought in Germany as Lessing and Kant.

In large land-masses there is a tendency for culture to be dominated by provincial centres. One of the most important of the south-west German centres ever since the Middle Ages had been the city of Frankfurt am Main. The fact that the original city was founded on this site underlines its strategic situation at the crossing of several trade-routes; its market fairs were renowned throughout Western Europe from the thirteenth century. It was thus an obvious choice to become an Imperial Free City, one of those municipalities with a burgher class strong enough to take over complete responsibility for the management of their own internal affairs. Moreover, the importance of Frankfurt was underlined when it became the city designated as the theatre of each new emperor's coronation. Tradition required a new emperor to receive his consecration in Charles the Great's ancient cathedral at Aachen; but he at once proceeded from there to stage his secular coronation in Frankfurt. (The central position of the city within western Germany was once more brought out in the late 1940s when it was nearly chosen as the political capital of what is now the German Federal Republic. This central and socially prominent position was recognized equally at the end of the sixteenth century; for example, the Emperor Maximilian, striving, for the last time as it turned out, to unify his centripetal empire, created an Imperial court of final appeal, the Reichskammergericht, and housed it in the tiny Taunus township of Wetzlar, only a score of miles from Frankfurt.)[3]

It will be seen, therefore, that to be born in Frankfurt was indeed to be a citizen of no mean city. Goethe was, moreover, born into a well-to-do professional family. His parents were not amongst the very foremost citizens of the Imperial Free City, but he had numbered wealthy mayors of the city amongst his immediate forbears; indeed his family is very mixed, as might be expected the German middle class, which must have been mobile in order to get on. Some of his ancestors came from central Germany, the thriving industrial towns of western Saxony. Amongst these are said to have been the great painter Lucas Cranach, the contemporary and painter of Luther. More to the point, his lively and outspoken mother came from an innkeeper's family, an inheritance which contributed to keeping her son's feet firmly on the ground. This background of solid middle-class

[3] These facts are mentioned because they are all connected with events in Goethe's life. One might add that the first German elected assembly met at Frankfurt in 1848 in the Paulskirche. On Frederick the Great there is a vast literature. For a controversial but stimulating modern view see R. Augstein, *Preussens Friedrich und die Deutschen* (S. Fischer 1968). On the effects of 'Western' thought in Germany there are many sources. I prefer to follow the brilliant (if in places outdated) *Geschichte der deutschen Literatur im 18. Jh.* by H. Hettner (Leipzig 1921), and the difficult but generally wise *Geist der Goethezeit*, Vol. I, by H. A. Korff (Leipzig 1923, reprinted 1954). A thoughtful brief contribution is W. von den Steinen, *Das Zeitalter Goethes* (Sammlung Dalp, Berne 1949). On Frankfurt and the importance of geographical factors in German development I am prepared to follow a great deal in J. Nadler, *Literaturgeschichte der deutschen Stämme und Landschaften* (revised edns 1923–8, 1938–41), whilst discounting the general 'blood-and-soil' flavour of Nadler's conclusions.

wealth had allowed his father to study Law and to remain almost a gentleman of leisure as one who specialized in Imperial Constitutional Law and who was in consequence only infrequently called on for his opinion. Despite his title of Imperial Counsellor, Goethe's father only counted amongst the second rank of burghers in the city. Rank was nicely regulated in Frankfurt by the prescription of the number of candles which might be carried in lanterns by those who stirred abroad after nightfall. In the absence of street lighting all had to carry lights; but only very aristocratic nobles were allowed a lantern of three candles; the middling sort were allowed two and the ordinary masters one. The common people travelled by the light of other people's lanterns or did not stir abroad at all.

Though Frankfurt was a prosperous city, in 1750 it could not be compared with George III's London. One of the significant facts about the revival of Germany after the religious wars is that this revival favoured the land and cities of the north and east at the expense of those of the south and west. These latter had been the traditional home of German culture: if we speak today of High German, it is precisely because from the time of Charles the Great to the religious wars the centre of gravity of German culture was on High German soil, in the south and west. But from the time when German colonization of central Europe started, in the later Middle Ages, through to the age of Luther (who came from Eisenach, in eastern Germany), there are signs that a new German culture would one day spring up in the east. The devastation of the south and west during the religious wars gave the rest of Germany its chance. Thus though Martin Opitz (a Silesian) formed his first circle of lyric poets at the university of Heidelberg (in the south-west) in the first decade of the seventeenth century, the remainder of the development of what is today called 'baroque' poetry in Germany goes north and west, to Hamburg, to Berlin and Königsberg and, above all, to Silesia.

This development continued in the eighteenth century, especially with the rise of Prussia underlining the growth of Berlin as a major capital city. Moreover, Hamburg and the Baltic ports which were in close and ever-growing commercial contact with the British Isles profited from this to absorb much from the

English literary revival of the eighteenth century (and notably from the facets of that revival reflected in their particularly close neighbours in Scotland).[4] Thus it was not surprising that in the first half of the eighteenth century a group of poets came together in the north and began to scratch together a humus of culture. From this group emerged the first poet to be read and admired without reservation all over Germany, Friedrich Gottlieb Klopstock from Quedlinburg in the Harz Mountains. He was educated at the patrician grammar school at Pforta in Saxony and spent the rest of his life in Copenhagen and Hamburg.

Klopstock's first success came with the publication in 1748 (just a century after the Peace of Westphalia) of the first three cantos of his religious epic *Der Messias*, based no doubt on the work of Milton, but none the less a landmark in the revived self-confidence of young German poets at this period. It is difficult today to understand the peculiar appeal of Klopstock's pious verses; our intellectual climate has changed so much that we have little use for epic poetry in such quantities or of such specific density. That others do appreciate poetry of this sort is clear: even in our own day we have seen, for example, the success amongst the Russians of Tvardovski's *Vassili Tvorkin*, and amongst Spanish Americans of Pablo Neruda's *Canto General*. Though one may compare its effect to some extent with the success of Eliot's longer poems, there is no doubt that the pious tone of the whole, which is particularly tedious to the modern reader, was one of the main elements in Klopstock's success. There was no generation gap in the 1750s between parents and young over what they believed. Indeed there is every indication that Goethe's father, a student of the *philosophes* of the French Enlightenment, would have had less sympathy with Klopstock's edifying religious sentiments than his son.[5] For young Goethe

[4] Described in general by R. Pascal in *The German 'Sturm und Drang'* (Manchester 1968), and in greater detail in the same author's 'Herder and the Scottish Historical School', *Proceedings of the English Goethe Society*, Vol. IV (1939), pp. 23–42.

[5] Brilliantly covered, to my mind, by Edith Braemer in the first and last sections of her *Goethes Prometheus und die Grundpositionen des Sturm und Drang* (Weimar 1968).

was fed by his mother on the liveliest of contemporary religious writings, notably the effusions of the Pietists, and played the clavichord at their prayer-meetings in her *salon*.

There are strong links between the growing German eighteenth-century Pietism and the emergence of a new high-powered literary style. What Pietism gave to Germans seeking something more than the strait-laced orthodoxy of the state churches was an individual religion. There had, of course, been reformers to the 'left' of Luther, *Schwärmer* and Anabaptists: in so far as they attempted to defy the Lutheran orthodoxy of the time they were often eradicated by the sword. They persisted, as the astonishing phenomenon of the Münster 'communist' outbreak of 1534 testifies. Driven underground during the religious wars, they emerged afterwards as 'conventicles', isolated cells grouped only in the loosest fashion but with the toughness of the spider's web. It was his acquaintance with two model missionaries from the so-called 'Moravian' church which converted the worldly Anglican John Wesley, when he was shipwrecked off the American coast. And that there was a wide-flung Pietist organization is also clear from the American activities of one of the leading early eighteenth-century Pietists, Count Zinzendorf. It was on Zinzendorf's Saxon estate of Herrnhut that one of the most active congregations grew up from which missionaries went all over Germany; one finds 'Moravians' (called in German Herrnhuter) amongst Klopstock's friends in Hamburg as well as amongst the Swabian households in which during this period there grew up such dissimilar allies as Wieland and Schiller. Goethe was less exposed to Pietist influence than many, but it struck him at a particularly susceptible (teenage) period of his life and left an impression which, perhaps fortunately, was never to be eradicated. It may be noted that the young Goethe received from his mother's aristocratic Pietist friend, Susanna von Klettenberg, the manuscript of a conventional 'confession' in the form of an autobiography; on this he was many years later to base the transitional chapter of *Wilhelm Meister*, the 'Confessions of a Beautiful Soul'.

One final touch is necessary to complete this portrait of Goethe's background. In 1756 the Seven Years War broke out.

In the course of this war almost the whole of Germany was to be occupied at one point or another by foreign forces. It so happened that Frankfurt was occupied by the French and a senior French officer was billeted on the Goethe family. This might be said to have put the finishing touch to the French rococo influences playing on the young Goethe's mind. Amongst the most obvious of these one may recall the fact that during this period Goethe's father completely remodelled his large but still traditionally half-timbered city house and turned it into one of those pediment-topped neo-classical houses typical of the eighteenth century. In the entourage of the literature-loving Comte de Thoranc the young Goethe heard rococo literature discussed and even witnessed the performance of French plays in the manner of the original French classical theatre. It is not surprising, after that, to find Goethe's father deciding to send him at the age of 16 to the university of Leipzig, the most Frenchified of all the contemporary German institutions of higher learning.

When the Goethe home was redecorated it was given the style which can be seen today in the painstaking reconstruction now standing in the Hirschgraben in Frankfurt. The visitor will note that for all the superficial 'French' elegance of the rococo façade and wall decorations, the floors and staircases are redolent of a solid middle-class comfort; it reminds one of similar facets in eighteenth-century painting, where the domesticity of a Chardin and a Lancret descends in direct line from the opulence of the golden age Dutch painters Vermeer and de Hooch. If one looks at the decorations one discovers a certain panel which is dominated by picturesque Roman ruins, such as had been made fashionable by Hubert Robert and Poussin; seated on fallen columns are the elder Goethe and his wife (in contemporary fashionable attire!). They are surrounded, however, by *pastoral* symbols, notably sheep, which are also absorbing the attention of their two young children. As a symbolic representation of the 'influences' which affected the teenage Goethe, this panel cannot be bettered.

Chapter 2

Leipzig and Rococo

Why was the eastern city of Leipzig the most 'Frenchified' city of eighteenth-century Germany? The answer is: as a result of the power politics of the day. Saxony had been the home of the German Reformation, its dukes the protectors and executors of Luther's break with Rome. But in the century following the decisive break economic power slipped further and further away from the mines and looms of Saxony. By the time the religious war broke out in 1618 the former military frontier province of Brandenburg-Prussia was already beginning to grasp the lead amongst the Protestant states.[6] Prussia was a large land-mass but its thin sandy soil did not reveal its economic potential until the beginning of the seventeenth century when England, the country of the nascent Industrial Revolution, turned to its eastern neighbour for agricultural produce. As the exploding population of the British Isles ceased to be able to feed itself with its own corn and cattle, its political leaders looked round for imports of these – and found them in the Baltic. The resulting economic links were at their strongest during the Seven Years War in the eighteenth century when England helped Frederick powerfully during his seemingly hopeless struggle against the traditional Continental great powers.

The political tension between Prussia and Saxony was made strikingly apparent during the course of the Thirty Years War,

[6] Despite some modern work, the two most thorough general histories remain: F. L. Carsten, *The Origins of Prussia* (Oxford 1968) and S. B. Fay, *The Rise of Brandenburg: Prussia to 1788* (Holt, Rinehart & Winston 1965).

when there was time and again a strong suspicion of dragging of feet about the support given by the Saxon dukes to the Protestant side. This is particularly noticeable in the notorious tergiversations of the minor but locally important military leader Duke Bernhard of Sachsen-Weimar. On balance the Saxons could be counted amongst the Protestant leaders; but not long after peace had been restored the Elector of Saxony finally gave way to his House's secret desires and became a convert to Catholicism. This striking reversal of form was not the result of a popular movement and led to no great backsliding amongst the population. But for the Saxon royal house it did provide an entrée into the charmed circle of Roman Catholic aristocracy. Saxon princes and princesses became marketable properties for eligible French, Italian and Polish royal scions. As the ultimate outcome of this blood-link, at the beginning of the eighteenth century a Saxon Elector was finally elected King of Poland. The Polish kingship was at the mercy of an anarchic political system with roots deep in the troubled history of that unhappy country. In the seventeenth and eighteenth centuries it acquired a relative stability which was backed up by constant marriage ties with the French royal family. By entering into this circle the Saxons thus found themselves moving ever closer to the French.

Whilst the fame of Louis XIV still made France the leading country in Europe this was a great support. The political system of 'enlightened' despotism embodied in Louis XIV's system entailed the constant furthering of massive public buildings in order to impress the minds of the populace. These monarchs blatantly glorified themselves and their system in great buildings and splendid public works of art; thus it is not surprising to find that the Saxon rulers spread a blanket of French 'Versailles' taste over their electorate and its outriders. There is a palpable network of rococo art-history to be studied in the main centres of this eighteenth-century political alliance, ranging from rococo Italy through the France of Louis XV and Louis XVI to Dresden (the capital of the Saxon Electors) and Cracow and Warsaw (their Polish centres), and from there back to Nancy (given as an apanage to the exiled Polish king Stanislas Leszinski, Louis XV's father-in-law).

The French culture thus imported into Saxony could not but be a pervasive influence in Leipzig, economic capital of Saxony and seat of one of the oldest German universities. It was not simply to be noted in architecture and fashion, though it was plain enough there; it spread deeply into the very teaching of the university. The most striking sign of this may be seen in the slavish devotion to the French seventeenth-century neo-classical theatre which was preached by Leipzig University's most famous and perhaps hardest-working eighteenth-century professor, Johann Christoph Gottsched. Gottsched was an East Prussian; he had taken refuge in Saxony because, as a youth more than six feet tall, he feared conscription into the army of Frederick II's grandfather who had a fad for collecting six-footers to serve in his Guards.

The young Goethe came to this rococo university when it was completely dominated by the new fashion. Gottsched had been in his Chair for twenty years and his constant publicistic activity had completely won the public to his views. There is a well-known story of how he had, for example, collaborated with the Neuber theatrical troupe in solemnly banishing the old 'popular' theatre from the boards – even though the attempt of the combined forces of Gottsched and Frau Neuber to establish Racine and Corneille and the eighteenth-century imitators of Versailles classicism had not been popular enough to enable the widow Neuber to maintain her troupe in Leipzig as a standing theatre. Although we can follow the development of neo-classical rococo fashion in Germany in the mid-eighteenth century, it is always necessary to recall that the foreign influences 'in the air' were never unadulterated: thus amongst the French influences there were the oppositional voices of the radical *philosophes* to be found side by side with the orthodox works of Louis XIV's writers. And, parallel with these, and possibly overwhelming them at times, were the works of the writers of the contemporary English Enlightenment, whose 'little magazines' (the *Tatler*, the *Spectator,* etc.) enjoyed considerable popularity in Germany from the 1740s when the first German imitations were launched in Hamburg, the port where the merchants brought them in. Gottsched himself found the little magazines an indispensable weapon in his publicistic activity and he used them, in the sense defined by Lenin much later, as 'collective organizers' of his own 'language societies'.

In seventeenth-century France much of the publicistic activity of spreading literary knowledge was undertaken by the *salons*, an aristocratic form of social activity which became so popular that they ultimately were a kind of neutral forum where ideas were bandied about amongst the educated middle class as well as the aristocracy. In Germany Gottsched attempted to achieve synthetically what had been spontaneous expressions of the social life of Versailles and Paris; moreover, in the absence of a centralized court as all-embracing as was the court of France, his *salons* (the 'language societies') were much more likely to be composed of educated bourgeois than of aristocrats. Nevertheless, it is important to emphasize the essentially aristocratic slant of this culture: many of Gottsched's pupils and emulators were indeed of noble birth (J. E. von Schlegel, E. von Kleist, and K. W. von Borcke, to name a few important figures almost at random). The ambience of this culture was still as class-bound as was the governance of Germany. Again, almost at random, one may note the importance of, for example, the patronage of the King of Denmark (as Duke of Schleswig-Holstein a prince of the Holy Roman Empire) for the development of Klopstock's genius, and the patronage of Count Stadion (Chancellor of the Archbishop of Mainz, himself Chancellor of the Empire) for Wieland's career and work.[7] Above all it is necessary to point to the quite exceptionally important place of the royal families of Braunschweig-Wolfenbüttel and Sachsen-Weimar in the culture of the eighteenth-century Germany.

The royal family of Wolfenbüttel had long had a tradition of interest in literature. At the end of the sixteenth century its duke Heinrich Julius was one of the more successful practitioners of the post-Luther school of dramatic writing. In the next generation its duke Anton Ulrich wrote some of the most influential

[7] Because it presents the story in the sociological terms which I am attempting to use I quote here my own *C. M. Wieland*, Harrap 1961.

'political' novels of the baroque genre. The tradition was constantly maintained and we are not surprised to find that it was a Wolfenbüttel duke who employed Lessing as court librarian in the last phases of the great writer's career. But the most significant event of all was to be the wedding of a Wolfenbüttel princess, Anna Amalia, to the heir apparent of the Duchy of Sachsen-Weimar.

This branch of the Wettin dynasties had not the same tradition of creative intervention as the Brunswick royal family. But the Wettin courts were, for example, the scene of Johann Sebastian Bach's early creativity at the beginning of the eighteenth century. Anna Amalia came to a court where civilized pursuits were rather more the fashion than was normal amongst the minor German princes (whose self-indulgence in the excesses of the flesh was notorious all over Europe).[8] Moreover she was not only widowed young but left with two young sons to whose education she determined to devote the rest of her life. It was this pursuit which led her to invite the most sophisticated of contemporary writers to Weimar as the young Karl August's tutor. Wieland proved a hopeless educator and another (and much more solid) promising man of letters, K. L. von Knebel, had to be introduced to pursue the training of the prince and his younger brother. But Wieland's literary influence remained predominant in the court, and was still strong when Karl August invited the new young lion of the German literary scene, the young Goethe, to pay him a visit which was ultimately to make Weimar the intellectual and spiritual capital of Germany for nearly two centuries.

All this was still a decade or more away, however, when the 16-year-old Goethe arrived in Leipzig in 1765. But the lively youngster soon showed signs of a development more sophisticated than that of his contemporaries. Although the *opuscula* of his two Leipzig years do not rise far above those of the many poetasters flourishing in this gay city, they begin to show a sure grasp of the demands of real literature. Apart from a handful of gay and spirited letters to friends and family, they comprise

[8] See the mass of material presented rather sensationally in A. Fauchier-Magnan, *The Small German Courts in the 18th century* (Methuen 1958).

above all some promising verses and two small plays which still bear studying.[9]

In starting his literary career with verse and plays Goethe was following exactly the trend of rococo literary fashion. Today, although it is still possible for a would-be writer to make his debut with dramatic works, and although there are still some writers who first make their mark (though with increasing infrequency) in the field of verse, it is in prose that most literary beginners feel that they have to shine. In the eighteenth century, as in all previous centuries since the Renaissance, the order was reversed. Literature, for most people concerned with it (and they were, be it noted, always the minority), meant above all poetry; poetry was read aloud in the *salons* and perused in study and boudoir. All men of importance with literary leanings considered it necessary to be able to write passable verse, were they diplomats or soldiers, merchants or scientists: Hagedorn, passable writer of rococo trifles, was a diplomat, Kleist a soldier, Brockes and Gessner (perhaps the most widely known of German writers at the time Goethe was a Leipzig student) merchants, and Haller a scientist (also of European renown).

Prose was still far from being the most sought-after medium in which to gain fame. Wolfgang Kayser[10] has pointed out that by the end of the eighteenth century the novel, which in 1700 represented only a very small proportion of the literature being printed, formed the bulk of published works. Yet half-way through the century the change had barely begun: more writers than ever were, it is true, turning out novels, but these were still considered to be on a level with the journalistic products sold at the village fair. Where in previous centuries the barely literate populace had been regaled with chap-books and broadsheets, there was a growing tendency to supply it with fully fashioned

[9] The most easily available collections of Goethe juvenilia are in the volume of *Dt. Lit. in Entwicklungsreihen* ed. Kindermann called *Der Rokoko-Goethe* (Leipzig 1932), and, of course, the standard six-volume collection by M. Morris, *Der junge Goethe* (original edn 1909–12). Since 1965 this has been in process of being re-edited by E. and R. Grumach.

[10] In 'Die Anfänge des modernen Romans', *Deutsche Vierteljahresschrift*, Vol. 28 (1954), p. 417.

novels. But even the form of these had still not set: some followed the baroque vogue of largely shapeless picaresque adventure-stories. Some took the form of alleged collections of letters; many of these not only took their form from the English pioneer Richardson, but also used Richardson's introduction of the sentimental love-story as their model. There was also a trend towards using this new form for edifying purposes, employing either a kind of Sunday-school story-telling mixed with heavy moralizing or moving the novel close to those pamphlet-style satirical writings which had also long been in vogue at the fairs. All these genres had their adepts by the mid-century and were known at the university of Leipzig where the Professor of Latin, Gellert, had earned perhaps the greatest popular acclaim within Germany with his sentimental and moral novel *Leben der schwedischen Gräfin von G.*,[11] and the Professor of Law, Rabener, was known to wield a deft satirical pen.

Goethe did not have the maturity to imitate them at this stage in his career, but this was the ambience of the first observations which were to lead him within a very few years to the writing of the novel *Werther*, which was to earn him undying fame in the whole of Europe. For the moment he was observing and recording with mordant wit in his private correspondence. He was also gaining increased knowledge of the world in his contact with other students and in his social life. The old romantic biographies used to record an affair in Leipzig with an innkeeper's daughter. The truth is that Käthchen Schönkopf, the object of his affections, was, like his mother, the offspring of a wealthy innkeeping family, and a (comparatively) sophisticated young lady of impeccably 'Frenchified' taste who moved in a quite elevated social sphere which included, amongst others, the children of the family of Breitkopf, the music publishers, a distinguished Leipzig concern.

But it was neither his rococo dallying nor his social observation (which led to the scene with the students in Auerbach's Cellar

[11] There is an interesting note by F. Bruggemann in his edn of the novel in *Dt. Lit. in Ent.* (Leipzig 1933). I have just written one of the few studies of it in contemporary terms; the article will shortly appear in *Orbis Litterarum* (Copenhagen).

in the germinating *Urfaust* drama) which may be said to have been the most productive thing to which Goethe turned his attention in Leipzig. It is said too, and not without some likelihood of its being true, that the curious figure of the sardonic Mephistopheles owes more than a little to the freshman Goethe's acquaintance with a high-spirited older student called Behrisch, a worldly-wise second-year student with whom Goethe was to maintain a lifelong friendship when the other man became tutor to one of the Wettin ducal families. What was of great importance for his development was his resolution to turn to painting, and the lessons which he took from a celebrated Leipzig professor of Art, Adam Oeser. Oeser played a considerable role in the history of the revival of neo-classical art in Germany at this point in the century; he was a friend and correspondent of the greatest of the German art-critics of the century, Johann Joachim Winckelmann, a man who was to play an important part in the gradual turn towards neo-classicism of Goethe's tastes. In taking up this acquaintance Goethe was not only developing his own powers of observation; he was also throwing out a line to one of the major sources of strength in the developing arts of the time.

In becoming Oeser's pupil Goethe was not only fostering his latent talents as an artist; he was to learn the neo-classicists' devotion to the arts of ancient Greece and Rome. He was very much in the fashion of the times, of course; and the first seeds of this interest had doubtless been sown by his father's neo-classicism, a product of the Enlightenment, that taste which led the elder Goethe to 'modernize' the family home and to collect Classical busts and coins. And the mixture of styles, already described, infected both the interior decoration and the Hirschgraben house and Gottsched's own literary innovations. Oeser, too, was no mere imitator of Roman forms; in his development the realistic art of Dürer and the domestic naturalism of the Dutch and Flemish painters also played their role. The heritage of taste thus passed on to the young student was full of elements which could be indefinitely expanded into something new and attractive. There is even in the most challenging works of the young rebel Goethe in the 1770s an element of hankering for an idyllic bourgeois existence which may well owe a great deal to the lessons in artistic taste given him by Oeser. This hankering for the 'kleine Hütte', as it has been so perceptively disentangled by Willoughby,[12] is very noticeable in the lyric poetry of the next few years of his life; it is especially noteworthy in Faust's great monologue as he enters Gretchen's bedroom, where the sexual desire depicted so feverishly in earlier scenes with Mephistopheles is completely eclipsed by a lyrical joy at being enabled here to share in the loved one's domestic bliss. It was this feeling again which enabled the literary lion to settle with such astonishing speed and lack of friction into the rather humdrum domesticity of Weimar.

It must not be thought that domesticity was the keynote of Goethe's Leipzig years. He was by modern standards young to be a university student and he played a full part in the life of the university city. There must have been dark as well as brilliant passages in this life. Something went wrong with his apparently carefree existence. He fell ill, so desperately ill that when he finally reached his home in Frankfurt again his life was in danger. The collapse seems to have been mental as much as physical, though doubtless domestic life in the 1760s was desperately dangerous by modern medical standards. But Goethe ended his Leipzig career in a run-down condition and it was to take him a full year back at home for his health to return to normal.

[12] In many of his recent essays but notably in 'Literary relations in the light of Goethe's principle of *Wiederspiegelung*', *Comparative Lit.*, Vol. I, (1949).

Chapter 3

The Importance of Pietism

The city of Frankfurt in which Goethe grew up and to which he now returned was still largely a medieval one. Until they were bombed in the devastating raid of 1944 which almost entirely changed the face of the old city, whole streets could still be visited which had changed very little since the sixteenth century. The carved and painted half-timbered houses differed from the fourteenth- and fifteenth-century farmhouses still to be seen in the little towns along the river Main only in being rather larger, as suited the burghers of the local metropolis. Though wealthy and forward-looking individuals like Johann Kaspar Goethe might redecorate their homes in the more 'modern' neo-classical style, with neat rectangular windows under a domestic triangular pediment, the visual aspect of the city was still largely *altdeutsch*.

The streets too were traditional, narrow and irregular, twisting and often cavernous. The open places and squares were sudden interruptions of the streets, embellished with quaint fountains and strange monuments to a past with which the local families almost all had direct personal links. There was no street-lighting, but one can well imagine that under artificial lighting the general effect would have been as theatrical as it is today in the old quarter of Miltenberg and Amorbach.

To appreciate fully how much of this background to *Faust* was bred into Goethe by his home, it is necessary to recall that he had just passed two years in a very different atmosphere, in Leipzig, where the rococo taste of the Saxon court had made much more headway, and that he had visited Dresden, the residence of that court, a city which had been almost entirely rebuilt according to the neo-classical town-planning notions of international rococo. The young student would have been susceptible to the comparisons too, because his illness and depression turned his thoughts away from the worldly interests of his Saxon days and impelled him to take up a particularly 'medieval' aspect of the wave of religious revival which was beginning to sweep across Germany and western Europe. Not satisfied with the Pietism in which his mother was currently interested, he delved into very much older mystical works and spent hours instructing himself in the weird doctrines of cabbalists, Rosicrucians and alchemists. He even set up his own alchemical laboratory, whose effect, inside the cramped confines of the old Goethe home, must have been very much that of Faust's dusty Gothic study.[13]

We must beware of dismissing Goethe's alchemical studies as a mere contributory factor to the initial fascination with the occult which was ultimately to produce Mephistopheles and the more spooky side of his great drama. There is in the literature of alchemy much that is of lasting value. On the one hand the medieval alchemists and the pious cabbalists of the sixteenth and seventeenth centuries (notably Paracelsus) were edging towards a scientific view of the world: alchemy is the mother of modern chemistry and even the great Dr Priestley, the discoverer of atomic weights, spent more time on the mystical aspects of his 'science' than on what today might be called 'pure research'. Newton wrote just as many mystical and cabbalistic works as he did astronomical and mathematical treatises. So Goethe was not simply turning backwards in this new preoccupation: he was also going deeper into the secrets of the universe than very many of the more superficial illuminati whose sole Bible was Diderot or Voltaire. On the other hand there was in the religious questioning of the mystics a search for God and pure religion which also opened perspectives wider than many of those to be found in the cynicism of the French and the scepticism of the English. The humus of Goethe's own 'organic' view of life, and of his constant later preoccupation with metamorphosis and growth (which makes him one of the precursors of Darwin), is the still muddled thinking of these Frankfurt days.

[13] See *Goethe the Alchemist*, R. D. Gray (Cambridge 1952).

Some direction was given to these hectic investigations by the contact with his mother's Pietist circle. The Goethe household was a normal well-to-do German upper middle-class eighteenth-century one: this means that the head of the household, Johann Kaspar, was not in the least interested in normal religious practices. Like most of the well-read illuminati, Goethe senior was a deist of an agnostic persuasion. This attitude, tolerant but fundamentally uninterested in Christianity, was spread through the family. But the lively mother of the household (in whom Goethe, in his famous quatrain, noted above all the '*Lust zu fabulieren*') must have felt chilled in this over-intellectual stratosphere. Amongst the many quixotic undertakings of her life, we cannot at this period discount her interest in Pietism.

Pietism is of outstanding importance for the development of German literature in the eighteenth century. The country of the Reformation was never entirely at home in the rationalistic world of the Enlightenment. Moreover in Germany, much more even than in England, the Lutheran pastorate formed a very large part of the educated population. One of the astonishing facets of the German *Aufklärung* is its close personal links with the pastorate: Herder, Lavater, Claudius and Gellert were all themselves ordained ministers; Lessing and Fichte were sons of the manse, whilst Wieland numbered many high church dignitaries amongst his ancestors and immediate family. The high moral tone of eighteenth-century German literature possibly even stems from the fact that these lost sons of religious leaders would, under different circumstances, have become pastors themselves; and they occupied themselves so intensively with ethics as being the nearest approach to preaching that an aggressively secular culture offered them. Schiller, it may be noted, too, was intending to take Holy Orders when his authoritarian ruler ordered him into his college to study Medicine.

There is no great eighteenth-century German writer who does not show some acquaintance with Pietism at some stage in his upbringing. In Goethe's case it was slighter than most. His mother's passing flirtation with Pietism went little further than the reading of pious books and the holding of prayer-meetings in her drawing-room, at which the returned student accompanied the hymns on the clavichord. But even these hymns were interesting for the emotional growth of a lyric poet. Much of the soul of a century otherwise dedicated to rationalism went into them; into the hymns, moreover, passed the spirit of that abortive flight of lyrical genius which manifested itself in the poets' circles of the early seventeenth century. The immediate heir of Opitz and Gryphius was the great Lutheran hymn-writer Paul Gerhard, and his inheritance passed in the eighteenth century via Bach and his text-writers to such poets as the Saxon Count Zinzendorf. Sickly and often rebarbative as their writings seem today, there was in this religious poetry a feeling for language and a desire to communicate feeling which was good pabulum for nascent lyric writers.

Altogether Pietism was a favourable seed-bed for the new literature. The orthodox Lutheran Church had become very sterile indeed: there were times when many pastors would devote all their sermons to giving their flocks lessons in seed-cultivation or animal husbandry. Their Bible-exposition was of the driest order. Small wonder that conventicles of believers, dissatisfied with this, came together to study the Bible for themselves and to indulge, in the warmth of a small friendly circle, in more expansive religious exercise. This kind of subterranean religious exercise is seen at its most productive in the work of the Silesian cobbler Jakob Böhme. Böhme not only wrote mystical works which were carried to many parts of Germany by his wandering artisan adherents; he also wrote hymns and stimulated others to follow his example. Part of the mystical theology of the Pietists (this general name cannot be applied to any single religious grouping) was the desire to share their religious experience; this stimulated the shy to participate and also gave them something to say – for who has not had some religious experience, especially when living in a fundamentally hostile environment? From this desire to communicate there also stemmed a practice of open confession (still maintained by revivalist movements today). Such confessions might be trite, but they represent a blind groping towards the objective study of the human personality: just as alchemists were groping towards chemistry, so the Pietists were groping towards psychology.

Amongst the better educated converts (and it should be remembered that the bulk of the members of conventicles were almost illiterate except for their Bible-study) such confessional practices often took the form of written autobiography. It may well be that the growing market for prose fiction in the eighteenth century is not unconnected with the Pietist interest in real autobiographical confession.[14] The chap-book and the broadsheet had always shown an interest in crude moralizing about outstanding murders and other violent happenings. This was eagerly seized on by propagandist writers in the first half of the century, who produced novels only slightly more elevated than the broadsheet. Where a genuine Pietist could take up this literary form, the modern psychological novel was almost unveiled: the pious (but not Pietist) Gellert enthralled all Germany with his *Leben der schwedischen Gräfin von G.*, a mixture of bizarre adventure and solid moralizing; the Pietist Karl Philipp Moritz wrote an autobiographical novel of confession, *Anton Reiser*, which is an admirable prelude to the modern psychological novel; whilst one of the best friends of Goethe's next few years, Heinrich Jung-Stilling, was to achieve lasting celebrity with his simple Pietistic autobiography. The Pietists made Germans aware that they were individuals: if we talk of the great demythologizing service of the Age of Reason, we must say that this was its culminating point. But the wresting of the ego from the collective anonymity of a medieval theology was not the work of the illuminati, it was the work of the Pietists.

Goethe had one concrete example of this in his mother's circle. He was befriended by an aristocratic middle-aged lady, Susanne von Klettenberg, who became an intimate companion of his mystical and alchemical studies. She even lent him her own written autobiography, and the impressionable student was deeply moved – so moved, in fact, that when, years later, he was looking for ways in which to turn a youthful novel, overweighted in the direction of Sturm und Drang revolt, into a broader picture of the emergence of a human personality, he fell back on Fräulein von Klettenberg's autobiography and reproduced its essence, in the form of the 'Bekenntnisse einer schönen Seele', as the chapter

[14] See *Design and Truth in Autobiography*, R. Pascal (Oxford 1968).

which forms the bridge between the first version of *Wilhelm Meister* and the more mature chapters.

We do not know how much of the 'Bekenntnisse' is genuine, in the sense of being actually taken from the original 'autobiography'. Even if it is all invented, the difference in tone between this chapter of Goethe's great novel and what precedes it shows how different are the sources from which the two sprang. It is doubtful if even a writer with the imaginative grasp of a Goethe could have totally invented this story of a young aristocratic girl who draws more and more away from the superficial gaiety of a worldly court life as she matures. Generations of Goethe critics have assumed the confessions to be authentic because the point of view is totally feminine. The attitude is also aristocratic in a way which could not have been natural to the bourgeois (this contact, it may be noted, would also have helped the poet later to make his way in the courtly world of Darmstadt and Weimar).

Naturally Goethe did not simply drop the 'Bekenntnisse' into his novel like a stone into a pond. He reworked parts of the early novel to prepare for it, and he used some of the characters whom he brought into the confessional story for the later development of the plot. But the fact that he remembered his mother's Pietist friend demonstrates how deeply must have been the impact made on him at this period of his life.

As soon as he had recovered from his illness and was once more restored to a youthful vigour which had been considerably enriched by this return to his home, Goethe was once more packed off to the university. But not to Leipzig. His father doubtless felt that the rococo air had not been an unmixed blessing. Why he should have chosen to send him to a university which was almost the exact opposite of Leipzig cannot be ascertained. For Goethe the polarity was certainly very useful. Strasbourg, to which he was now sent, was, of course, an old university and a famous one; at this stage, too, it had something of a name for promising science students. But, above all, it was remarkable in that it was as unrestrainedly and normally 'German' as Leipzig had been 'French' – and this despite (or perhaps because of) the fact that it was actually on French soil. Alsace had been French since its gradual absorption in the later seventeenth century by Louis XIV.

Chapter 4

The Shock of Strasbourg

It seems likely that Goethe was only intending to use Strasbourg as a staging-post on the way to visiting Paris; the ideas of the rococo were obviously still present in his mind. His father would undoubtedly not have looked with much favour on any announced departure from the canons of his Enlightenment faith. But the effect which the old capital city of Alsace was to have on the young student was something quite different and it may be seen from the very first moment when Goethe stood in the narrow square in front of the cathedral and gazed on its pink-hued Gothic massiveness.

As Goethe wrote soon after in a letter to a friend, this was something for which he had not been prepared. He had grown up under the influence of his father's French taste; nothing in the cramped Frankfurt of his youth prepared him for the overwhelming impact of the monumental Gothic style, as evidenced in Strasbourg Cathedral. St Nicolai's Church in Frankfurt is sober and unimpressive, and the main influence of Leipzig and Dresden in his student days would have been appreciation of the new French style of the buildings.

Intellectually, too, the Enlightenment which had been all around him in his early years looked down on the Gothic as a barbaric art form. It was indeed the Renaissance, with its worship of everything antique, which called the architecture of medieval Europe 'Gothic', using as a term of abuse the name of a Germanic tribe widely held to be responsible for the ruination of the Roman Empire it so admired. Thus Goethe's eyes would have been closed to the many beauties of the Gothic buildings which he must have passed on his journeyings east and west at this period.

Nor ought we to exaggerate (as the Romantic movement did) the fervour of his admiration for the Gothic qualities of Strasbourg Cathedral. Robson-Scott[15] has argued persuasively that many of the qualities of harmony and balance which Goethe stressed in his contemporary effusions on the cathedral to correspondents and interlocutors and in his later programmatic pamphlets are more explicable in terms of orthodox Classical aesthetics than in terms of the aims of the medieval builders. One may be justified in assuming that Goethe was carried away by the immediate impact of what is in any case a remarkable building (the unearthly pink tint of the stone, plus the close proximity to half-timbered houses which are more highly decorated than those in the Main region to which Goethe would have been accustomed), and especially by its size: it was much bigger than any building which Goethe had hitherto seen. The effect on him may therefore be compared, in some respects, to the effect of the Eiffel Tower on *fin de siècle* visitors to Paris or to the impact of the skyline of New York on provincial visitors unused to tall buildings.

None the less Goethe was impelled by his enthusiasm for the cathedral to think about the Gothic legacy in Germany. This return to a cultural style more indigenous than that of the international rococo (though, of course, Gothic is anything but an exclusively German building style) seems to have been a journey undertaken of his own volition. It is important because one of the most significant events of Goethe's stay in Strasbourg was his first meeting with Herder, and perhaps the most important idea which the latter passed on to his eager listener was the continuing inspiration of the medieval cultural heritage. If there is any further need for an explanation of this Gothic enthusiasm of the newly arrived student, it could perhaps be found in the aesthetic teachings of his Leipzig art master Oeser, whose predilection for the chiaroscuro of the Dutch and Italian baroque painters would have gone some way to prepare him to receive

[15] One of the most illuminating studies of the Sturm und Drang, even if it is from one angle only, is W. D. Robson-Scott's *The Literary Background of the Gothic Revival in Germany* (Oxford 1965).

with enthusiasm the grotesque ornamentation of such a specimen of High Gothic as Strasbourg.

Perhaps the most interesting side of Goethe's decisive residence in the Alsatian university town is the amount of activity the young man crammed into less than seventeen months. This covers particularly his academic work. Strasbourg's statutes were fiercely and rigidly French; Goethe, though not at all well prepared for higher legal study, plunged into the minutiae required of the Part One student and passed his examination in a very short space of time. This enabled him to proceed at his own speed to the submission of work for his licentiate's degree without having to attend stipulated courses of lectures or pass a given number of terms in residence. It was a peculiarly French arrangement which was not well understood in Germany, so that Goethe's father was dissatisfied when the young man returned in 1771 as a licentiate, and thought that he should have stayed at least until he was within sight of a doctorate, which was the normal procedure amongst academic lawyers. So little understood was the French procedure that posterity has often doubted Goethe's qualifications as a lawyer, whilst his own contemporaries were never quite sure whether or not he might be referred to as Dr Goethe (a form of address which, later on, gave him the successful professional man's usual thrill of pride).

In fact Goethe refused a suggestion made by the Law Faculty at Strasbourg University after his return to Frankfurt that he should return and complete his doctorate. He was never an eager Law student and realized, as he was to say within a few years of setting up in practice, that his legal talents were amongst his least glorious. Indeed his modest success in the academic world is all the more remarkable when one discovers how many distractions beset him during the course of these Strasbourg months. They began in his lodgings where he became intimate with a large and varied student and professional circle. Doyen of the group was an accountant in his forties whose spare time was spent in antiquarian activities (Rousseau's call for a return to nature was paralleled amongst the wider educated public by a growing interest in the 'primitive' – at first interpreted as meaning simply 'pre-Renaissance'). The fact that Herr Salzmann had the young

Goethe admitted to his *Deutsche Gesellschaft* was just as important for the latter's Germanophile activities during these years as was his enthusiasm for the cathedral: indeed the two enthusiasms were obviously complementary.

Several of the other students in Goethe's midday dining group were studying Medicine, the branch of learning for which the university was particularly notable. Goethe at once attached himself to them and followed his alchemical studies with frequent attendance at botanical lectures and anatomical dissections. Amongst the students there were two in particular who impressed him, a quiet and impressively genuine ordinand called Lersé, whose decency so haunted Goethe that he called one of the really 'good' characters in *Götz* after him, and a pietistic medical student rather older than the others called Heinrich Jung-Stilling. Stilling was by no means brilliant, but the fact that Goethe was so attracted to him is an indication that beneath the frothiness which made outsiders shake their heads about the young man from Frankfurt was a solid kernel. The persistence of the link with Pietism should be noted, especially as Goethe wrote to his Frankfurt patroness, Fräulein von Klettenberg, that he had tried to contact the local conventicles in Strasbourg and been repelled by their bigotry and narrow-mindedness.

Goethe's contact with the Church was not to stop here, however. One of his other fellow-students took him out riding to a village north of Strasbourg where his cousin was pastor. Sessenheim (the spelling 'Sesenheim' which is normally found in Goethe and Goethe-criticism is no doubt a result of his heavy Frankfurt accent) is one of the many almost flamboyantly *altdeutsch* villages of Alsace, and there is something slightly hagiographical about the way in which German legend and literary history have enshrined the memory of the pastor's daughter, Friederike Brion, in her peasant national costume. This is all the more suspicious since most accounts of Goethe's love for Friederike rest on the description Goethe himself gave of it in *Dichtung und Wahrheit*, and this passage is closely linked with a literary argument adducing Goethe's Strasbourg introduction to contemporary English literature and notably to Goldsmith's *The Vicar of Wakefield*. In fact, the only letter Friederike wrote to Goethe which is preserved is in French and penned with only rudimentary skill; our doubt as to the beauty and intelligence of the object of an undergraduate's deathless love is underlined by Goethe's own admission in his autobiography that he was taken aback by the figure she cut when he finally saw her in Strasbourg society rather than in the pastoral landscape in which he preferred to enshrine her for the purpose of hymning her.

The power of the *Sesenheimer Lieder* owes almost everything to Goethe's introduction to a new sort of poetry by the other great experience of his Strasbourg days, Johann Gottfried Herder. Of the first poems inspired by the student's 'rustic' love, 'Mit einem gemalten Band' is, despite a significantly original ending, essentially rococo still, with its ribbons and pink roses. The influence of Herder, however, was cataclysmic and was the propelling power which set Goethe off on his career of real greatness.

Herder was only five years older than Goethe when the student sought him out in his Strasbourg inn, but for young writers a gap of this size is enormous. Goethe was hardly known outside local circles, where he was considered to be a lively young man of some promise. Herder, though only recently arrived from eastern Europe, had already published several critical articles which had made his name in literary circles in western Germany. A very hard childhood and adolescence had not dismayed him and when he finally went to the university of Königsberg as an ordinand, he at once made his mark as a young thinker who would raise even higher the banner of East Prussian culture which had been unfurled in the 1750s and 1760s by such rising stars as Hamann, the eccentric man of letters, and Kant, the professor of Mathematics. Kant's disciplined thinking equipped Herder with a sound philosophical method, and Hamann's spirited interventions, published in countless privately printed pamphlets, directed his attention to contemporary literature. Herder's first theoretical studies in literary aesthetics were immediately taken up by the most influential literary circle in mid-century Germany, the Berlin group around the rationalist publisher Nicolai, the friend of Moses Mendelssohn and Lessing.

When he graduated from Königsberg Herder could look forward to a splendid career in the Lutheran Church. He was directed to a parish in the German community in the great Baltic port of Riga, where he was also appointed to teach at the high-powered Cathedral School. In Riga there was also a lively literary life and Herder continued his friendship with Hamann and the latter's lively and highly sophisticated patrician friend, the merchant Berends. But he too felt the need of the polish which it was assumed only France could give, and so he became tutor to two young Baltic noblemen from the von Kleist family who were setting out on the Grand Tour. He took ship through the Baltic, landed at Nantes and mixed with Enlightenment *salons* in Paris. There he was invited to take up a similar role with the son of the Prince-Bishop of Lübeck, who was also an admirer of his early critical work. He went to the Prince's court at Eutin in Holstein and was about to set out with his charge when he was assailed by a painful affliction of the eye. To cure this he was advised to undergo an operation which was the speciality of one of the famous Strasbourg professors.

This was the reason why he now crossed Goethe's path. The operation played a considerable role in the relationship between the two young men, for Herder had to spend many weeks in almost complete darkness and Goethe, eager to draw out the pundit, volunteered to keep him company, to read to him and to keep him occupied during his painful convalescence. This intensive course in contemporary literary theory was the most important academic undertaking of Goethe's Strasbourg year. For Herder was on the threshold of launching German literary theory on to new paths. Taking up where Lessing was leaving off, he was challenging the very foundations of Renaissance classical literary theory. Herder was probably all the more inclined to look in a bleakly objective way at Greece and Rome because he was a theologian: his devotion (itself not untouched by Pietist influences) to the Bible opened his eyes to other modalities of lyrical expression than the strictly formalized approach of the French neo-classical school. As a Königsberger he was also influenced by the work of such English critics as Blackwell and Young. The decisive turn may well also have been provided by the wealth of traditional poetry and folk-song available in Latvia, where a collection had already been made by the German pastor

Glock. Indeed, for one who was beginning to realize that literature could stem from direct inspiration without need for such rules as could be squeezed out of Aristotle and Horace, Latvia provided a fruitful atmosphere. In the busy port of Riga German culture amongst the middle and upper classes rubbed shoulders with fragments of Swedish and Russian culture imported by the great powers who ruled the city in turn in the seventeenth and eighteenth centuries. And in the background and all around in the countryside was the great wealth of traditional Lettish culture. Glock first and Herder later had here a field of folk-poetry much richer than the Scottish Lowland culture paradigmatically collected by Bishop Percy in his *Reliques of Ancient English Poetry*. Herder was not satisfied merely to study folk-poetry (it was actually he who coined the word *Volkslied*); he had not merely pointed to the Bible as a work of literature. His archaeological studies also interested him in drama – Luther, it may be noted, had in his own day suggested that the Apocryphal books of Judith and Tobias were originally respectively a tragedy and a comedy. This approach he had carried over into his studies of Shakespeare.

Herder was a magnetic personality brimming over with ideas which he expounded forcefully and eloquently. Goethe was spellbound: neither Shakespeare nor early poetry was unknown to him, but he had hitherto approached them with the critical kid gloves of the rococo. Suddenly new worlds opened up to him and through this the well-springs of his own creativity were unblocked. It is well known how he at once set about writing a dramatized version of an early sixteenth-century autobiography which he had previously studied during his alchemical days in Frankfurt. This first version of the story of the Knight of the Iron Hand was both wild and exaggerated, in its underlining of those 'pop' elements which Herder had just brought to his attention. Herder's stressing of Shakespeare's anti-classical dramatic form gave rise to a fragmentation of small scenes which, even in the two later versions of *Götz von Berlichingen*, made stage performance difficult for the primitive theatrical techniques of the eighteenth and nineteenth centuries. In his desire to stress the link between the theatre and popular culture, Goethe introduced gypsies, revolutionary peasants and rough soldiers regardless of the economy which stage performance under any circumstances requires. It is small wonder that when the completed product was finally shown to him, Herder could not forbear to criticize and, though recommending it to his fiancée, pointed out that there were many places in which the play was over-deliberately seeking to make an effect (*'obgleich hin und wieder es auch nur gedacht ist'*).

Herder's hard upbringing had made him over-sensitive in his personal relationships and he had already become dissatisfied with his (remarkably generous) treatment at the hands of the Prince-Bishop. He was therefore happy to receive, though by the mediation of his patron, a call to become pastor in Bückeburg in the service of his patron's friend, the Count of Schaumburg-Lippe. In the collection of Alsatian folk-songs sent after him by his grateful disciple was included the original on which Goethe based his deathless 'Heidenröslein'.

We can imagine how busy must have been Goethe's life in the early months of 1771 when all this fermentation was going on inside him. Despite the fact that he was deeply in love with Friederike and constantly riding backwards and forwards to Sessenheim (the poem 'Willkommen und Abschied' is the monument to this activity), we must realize that Friederike was not necessarily uppermost in his mind all the time. This caution is necessary to avoid over-estimating the sense of guilt Goethe would have felt at having to leave her when he finally passed his Law exams and decided in August 1771 to go back home. There must have been some sense of guilt (it was undoubtedly fed by the pathetic verses in which another of Goethe's Strasbourg fellow-students, the excitable Lenz, described the forlorn Friederike – to whom he also later laid siege); it may even have been that the pastor and his family did look on him as a presumptive son-in-law. The most important aspect of the relationship must be considered to be the shadow of guilt which it enabled Goethe in the next few years to cast on the loves of so many of his poetical heroes – Weislingen deserting Götz's sister Marie, Werther disrupting the engagement of Lotte, Clavigo's treatment of Marie Beaumarchais, the treatment of his wife by the hero of *Stella* and, finally, the complete insouciance with which Egmont shatters the bourgeois world of Klärchen and Faust the domesticity of Gretchen.

Götz had to be reworked in the comparative tranquillity of the next few years in Frankfurt; when it was published it at once established Goethe as the most promising new figure on the literary horizon. In the meantime the author returned to the fold as a successful graduate who had managed to make some valuable friends. The most important aspect of his university year in Strasbourg was the considerable widening of outlook which he had undergone and the mass of impressions which had rushed into his mind. Even though nothing of it was yet visible, a corner had been turned.

Chapter 5

Mirrors of Malaise

Goethe returned to Frankfurt and his father set him up in chambers as a practising lawyer. He was not an energetic practitioner and seems to have taken up fewer than three dozen briefs in the course of the next four years. Perhaps the most important happening in his legal experience was his attendance at the trial of a maidservant accused of infanticide.[16] This sordid episode undoubtedly triggered off the ultimate version of the Gretchen episode in *Faust* and through it the theme of infanticide became established as a particularly drastic and effective weapon in the dramatic arsenal of the young writers. These young men were, by the end of the decade, to be regarded as a 'school', even though the name Sturm und Drang was only later to be applied to them. It was taken from the title of a tragedy by Klinger, a close friend of Goethe's since the days when they had played together as children in the old city which was the background to the childhood of both men.

Although it must have been obvious to Johann Kaspar that his son was not wedded to the Law, he persisted in furthering Wolfgang's legal experience and persuaded him to spend a term in May 1772 at the Reichskammergericht in the nearby township of Wetzlar. This was convenient enough for Goethe, who was beginning to spread his wings and gain acquaintances in many different parts of Germany. He could scarcely have dared to

[16] The latest findings are neatly summarized in the introduction to *Urfaust*, ed. R. H. Samuel (London 1958). For an exhaustive and legalistic treatment of the problem of infanticide see J. M. Rameckers, *Der Kindesmord in der Lit. der Sturm und Drangperiode* (Rotterdam 1927).

dream that this visit was to lead him to write the novel which was to establish him as a European celebrity.

The Reichskammergericht was the supreme court of appeal of the Holy Roman Empire. Since the Empire was on its last legs (the final dissolution of the legal structure in the Act of Mediation of 1806 was merely the outward sign that Germany had outgrown the clumsy infrastructure accumulated rather than built over a thousand years), the court was not a dynamic centre. At the same time it did have an importance as a cog in the machinery of the Empire and was a lively social centre, the provinces of Germany all maintaining representative delegations there. For a young lawyer whose career could well have followed that of his father in the field of Constitutional Law, or for a young man looking for likely employment in some province's civil service, Wetzlar might be regarded as the usual kind of expensive finishing school.

Goethe looked forward to a stimulating vacation in this picturesque and hilly Taunus centre. As it happened, he had a sentimental affair with the fiancée of a young member of the Bremen delegation, J. C. Kestner, and made of it the most celebrated sentimental novel of the eighteenth century. Some critical points should be disposed of at once: Goethe may or, more probably, may not have been Werther; the important thing is that as a creative writer he made of the Werther situation a moving literary experience which became part of the imaginative life of countless young men and women of his own generation, as indeed of every generation since. Goethe was doubtless attracted to Lotte Buff, Kestner's fiancée, as he was attracted to many young women: indeed, one suspects at times that he was particularly attracted to them when they were already attached. In this period, for example, he also had a sentimental affair with a dark-eyed beauty, Maximiliane Brentano, which only ended when her husband forbade him to enter the house; of his later affairs one thinks notably of Frau von Stein and of the passionate poetry-writing flirtation with his friend's wife, Marianne von Willemer. There is, however, no need at all to equate Goethe with Werther. He was not heart-broken when the time came, after only a few months, to part from Lotte, and the idea of

D

presenting his hero as suicidal because of hopeless love is much more likely to have come to him after he had left Wetzlar; for it was then that he heard of the actual suicide of K. W. Jerusalem, another Wetzlar lawyer, an introverted young man from another delegation, whose suicide was the result of personal neuroses quite as much as it was the outcome of a hopeless passion for the wife of his chief. Above all, as Goethe himself said very apologetically to his close friend Kestner, the latter must not be equated with the rather stuffy Albert, the fictional fiancé of Werther's adored one. Albert had to be made to appear unattractive in order to establish an element of sympathy for Werther – all of which could scarcely have applied to Goethe's Gallic dallying with the real Lotte Buff.

Above all, however, the whole Werther story appears distorted if it is looked at solely as a tale of romantic heart-break. Werther tries to tear himself away from Lotte and joins the diplomatic service in one of the German provinces. But he is frustrated there by his bourgeois origins and so despairs of making any mark of his own in life that he returns to Lotte and unhappiness. This, as Lukacs[17] has stressed, is the specific Sturm und Drang fulcrum of the novel which has to be borne in mind. Goethe, it should be remembered, had still not made any mark of his own on the world; he had tremendous ambition, but there was little prospect in 1772 of his being able to achieve anything beyond what was within the grasp of any other of the young Wetzlar judges' 'devils'. One of his friends, the poet F. W. Gotter, a member of the Hanoverian delegation (Gotter was editor of the journal of the ebullient circle of poets at Göttingen University), suggested to him that he could get him a legal post in Hanover; Goethe's reply, though keeping all options open, was not really effusive: he realized that promotion as a bureaucrat was scarcely going to be swift. Even in Frankfurt the young lawyer was a very small fish in a large and well-stocked pond: it was this discrepancy between the talents he knew he possessed and the frustration

[17] On this aspect of *Werther* see G. Lukács, *Goethe und seine Zeit* (Berne 1947). A useful complementary study of the social aspects of the same novel is H. Schöffler, *Die Leiden des jungen Werther, ihr geistesgeschichtlicher Hintergrund* (Berlin 1938).

which was all he could see around him which was soon to make him – in defiance of parental disapproval – first become engaged to one of the wealthiest patrician heiresses in Frankfurt and then, abandoning his fiancée (Lili), take up an invitation to stay at a princely court.

It is also necessary to bear in mind the intellectual atmosphere amongst the young men whose acknowledged intellectual leader Goethe had become. This group of writers whom today we call the Sturm und Drang group was not a tightly knit coterie of the Parisian type – not least because German circumstances were vastly different from French. On Paris converged all the young men in France who wanted to make a name for themselves. Young Germans had no such magnetic centre (and were not to have one until the emergence in 1871 of Berlin as the Imperial capital). Even at this period we can discern only two focal points of literary development: one of these was the university of Göttingen in Hanover; the other, centred on the person of Goethe, fluctuated between Strasbourg (since Goethe spent 1770–1 there) and Frankfurt-Wetzlar-Darmstadt when he returned home.

There were many features common to both these groupings of young poets. Both groupings stress the fact that the members were indeed young. Mention has already been made of the fact that there was no generation gap between the young and their parents in this period. The young men grew up accepting the Enlightenment beliefs of the preceding generation, even though they might give vent to youthful sentiments somewhat more vociferously than their elders. And the youth of 1770 *did* take up their ideas in a somewhat more radical way than their fathers, not least because external events were facing them with moral issues more personally pressing than those which their fathers had faced in the fifties. By 1770 the theoretical appreciation of freedom implicit in the philosophies of the Enlightenment had begun to bear fruit in active political life in the American struggle for independence against the Hanoverian rulers of Britain, whilst in France the *ancien régime* was also felt to be entering its final phase. Social theories were beginning to take a more concrete form than they had done earlier in the daydreaming of Rousseau and Montesquieu. Thus in the orbit of the Göttinger Hainbund one finds the political radicalism of Gottfried August Bürger impinging on the Klopstockian poetical effusions of the Stolberg brothers and Gotter. That Goethe's group was also interested in the socio-political aspects of contemporary society is clear from the tragedies they produced: there was the astonishing radicalism of Lenz's *Die Soldaten* and *Der Hofmeister* as well as the critical attitude adopted by Goethe's Frankfurt admirers, Klinger and H. L. Wagner, in their infanticide dramas. Although contemporary critics tended to stress above all the Shakespearian strivings of these young dramatists, their social bitterness distinguished them quite sharply from the completely unpolitical Shakespearianism of literary predecessors such as the Holstein diplomat H. W. von Gerstenberg, or even Lessing, in his outline of a Faust tragedy.

To modern minds the plot of Goethe's novel may seem naïve. The frustration of Werther's career seems as trifling as the emotion generated by Werther's and Lotte's enthusiasm for Klopstock seems unmotivated. What cannot be gainsaid, however, is the very real emotional tension Goethe put into Werther's love of ordinary people, and especially the simple peasants whom he encounters on his sentimental wanderings. The attention which Goethe's magnificently lyrical writing focuses on descriptions of scenery as viewed through Werther's Ossian-drenched mind must not distract attention from the stories which emerge from the simple folk with whom he talks. These stories breathe a tremendous *and radical* sympathy for the underdog, which reaches a culmination in the depiction of Werther's social frustration as a would-be diplomat.

Just as the novel's ideas are obscured by the lyrical descriptions of scenery and Werther's love-declarations, so the direction of the whole work was obscured by the hero's suicide. The most penetrating of contemporary criticisms was Lessing's suggestion that Goethe should really have added a last chapter underlining his real meaning and *'je cynischer, desto besser!'* ('the more cynical it is, the better it will be'). Yet it was the lyricism of Werther as well as the sentimental love-story and its tragic outcome which carried it to a pinnacle of European fame. One is reminded by the novel's success of the fate of Shakespeare's tragedies, so often simply a vehicle for applause-seeking ham-actors, parading before audiences whose attention has been riveted to costumes and scenery (Nicolai observed bitterly that it was these last which probably attracted public attention when *Götz* was first performed in Berlin in 1774). Sentimentality was certainly in the air in this last third of the eighteenth century; the protagonists of the drama of the French Revolution undoubtedly saw themselves in Wertheresque rather than Marxist terms. On the most human level, suicide became so fashionable that government action had to be taken against the vogue in St Petersburg and London; but the spontaneous reactions of a whole generation, whose emotions were modelled on those of Werther and Lotte, carried the French Revolution into every corner of Europe. If this link is overlooked there remains only a story which is beautifully written but which is probably as morally ambiguous as so many uncommitted armchair critics living in less anxious times have declared it to be.

To Goethe the Werther episode was certainly only one aspect of his life in Frankfurt in October 1774. Other interests claimed him constantly. At the beginning of 1772 he had sent the first version of *Götz* to Herder and received in return his mentor's fundamental objections. Any possible depression was softened by a new friendship with another dynamic personality who opened up exciting possibilities, Johann Heinrich Merck, a high civil servant in the War Ministry of the adjacent Duchy of Hessen-Darmstadt. Merck, sometimes claimed to be the chief model for the urbane and witty Mephistopheles, was an inspiring talker and an excellent critic who took over the editorship of the expanding critical journal, the *Frankfurter Gelehrte Anzeigen*, in 1772. Through Herder's recommendation he visited Goethe, gained his friendship and won his collaboration as reviewer.

Herder had visited the court of Darmstadt on his Grand Tour with his pupils and had there become engaged to one of the Countess's ladies-in-waiting. Following the trend of the times, the Darmstadt court, inspired by the *Landgräfin* Karoline, had become enthusiastic adepts of the literary fashions. Though unaware of the deep subversive implications of the Sturm und Drang phase of Enlightenment thought, the court ladies and gentlemen participated to the full in its sentimental extravagances.

Merck was a consciously cynical master of ceremonies in these intellectual revels (he was later to commit suicide himself, and from motives which may not have been unlike those outlined above as the essential background to Werther's frustration). One of Goethe's occupations during these Frankfurt years was to hike over to Darmstadt at weekends and assist in the diversions; he paid sufficient attention here too to Caroline Flachsland to draw some jealous remarks from her absent fiancé, Herder, just working himself into his new position at Bückeburg.

But Goethe's main preoccupation during these years, from 1771 to 1774, was to set down on paper the ideas which had fermented during the seminal year in Strasbourg. *Götz* was recast in 1773 and, when published, was wildly acclaimed by the younger generation; the older generation saw its promise and some, like Wieland, were enthusiastic, though with reservations, whilst others, like Lessing, were mostly disturbed. Many lyrics were written and ultimately published, often in scattered 'little magazines'. The impetus was kept up even after the great success of *Werther*: thus *Clavigo* was published in October 1774 and also applauded, though the percipient Merck said that Goethe should not write conventional works of this kind but leave that to the others! As Goethe himself said later, Merck's advice was not entirely correct, since he did *not* pursue this vein – and the German dramatic repertoire has been all the poorer for it. Of the other dramatic works on his desk, *Stella*, equally conventional in form if not in content, was finished in 1774 (it was not printed until 1776), whilst at the same time *Faust*, *Egmont* and possibly even *Tasso* were taking shape.

All these works added together show the quality of the genius which was now at last gaining public recognition. It should be noted that the great works were constantly being interrupted by the production of occasional pieces for social occasions – now a literary parody, now a modernized version of the old Shrovetide comedy-form, now a rococo-like *Singspiel*, and always a stream of letters to friends (often containing the most famous of the lyrical poems), besides a considerable volume of reviewing for Merck's journal. Some of the articles which appeared in the journal were more than simple journalism; they included substantial theological contributions, showing notably Goethe's growing enthusiasm for the works of the seventeenth-century Jewish pantheistic philosopher Spinoza, to which he had just been introduced. In Spinoza Goethe found united a good many of the theological ideas which he had already encountered in a very diffuse way in the works of the alchemists. His kinship with such subjective attitudes to creation and human destiny was also nourished by his making the acquaintance of the Zürich Dean Lavater and the Düsseldorf amateur theologian Fritz Jacobi. Jacobi's gentle goodness impressed Goethe more than his theology, which seemed to him diffuse and wishy-washy. The relationship was a two-way one, for it is probable that Jacobi was influenced in the writing of his very popular sentimental novel *Woldemar* (1779), by reading the earliest version of *Wilhelm Meister*, which had also been started at this time and was sent for critical perusal to Jacobi's sensible wife Betty, another of Goethe's correspondents. Amongst the further feminine admirers with whom he exchanged ideas may be named the sister of the Stolberg brothers, Auguste, the object of a sentimental intellectual flirtation, and a distinguished and popular novelist, Sophie von Laroche, Wieland's early fiancée. She was a mature and romantic *grande dame*, now married to Count Stadion's natural son, and mother of the beautiful Maximiliane. It was Maxe who married the wealthy Frankfurt merchant Peter Brentano and carried on a flirtation with Goethe in 1773–4; she was the mother of the romantic poet Clemens and the sensational Bettina.

To round off the picture of Goethe's manifold intellectual and 'social' activities in these years it should be added that he journeyed up the Rhine to Düsseldorf to meet the Jacobis and then down the Rhine to Zürich and the Swiss Alps in the company of the brothers Stolberg. This last journey closes, as it were, the circle between the Göttingen and Frankfurt poles of the Sturm und Drang. In Zürich Goethe spent much time with Lavater, who was an energetic performer of good works in his parish, even though Goethe considered his Pietistic theology both hysterical and impractical; yet Lavater, like most men of the Enlightenment, is not defined simply as an other-wordly mystic. He was engaged at this time on a 'scientific' investigation into the connection between physiognomy and character. For this project it was easy to gain the interest of Goethe, who contributed a number of items to Lavater's well-produced series of physiognomical studies, which may well be called a kind of alchemical character-study and a forerunner of modern psychology. The number of copies still to be found on bookstalls testifies to its contemporary European fame.

The Swiss journey was somewhat feverish for Goethe and he stood at the top of the St Gotthard Pass and gazed in some perturbation of mind towards Italy. The reason for his distress was the fact that the whole journey was actually undertaken in order to give himself time away from the increasingly difficult situation in which he was finding himself in Frankfurt. Not the least of his worries was the fact that he had met Lili Schönemann and become engaged to her in a whirlwind courtship. Lili is the sole widely-acknowledged beauty amongst his feminine companions and, indeed, the one whom in his last years he held up as the girl whom he should have married. At this moment, however, he was thinking otherwise. Lili was not merely the 17-year-old daughter of one of the most patrician (and most wealthy) of the Frankfurt bankers; she was spoiled and entirely addicted to the social round of the *jeunesse dorée*. Goethe humoured her in this, though his feeling that he was being foolish added to his other worries. His deepest reason for concern was his growing unhappiness at the discrepancy between his fame (and his certainty that he could achieve even more), and the fundamental provincialism of life in Frankfurt even when lived on the highest social level. This high life was a source of discomfort to him from another quarter: his father's classical simplicity disapproved of 'debauchery' whilst his mother, otherwise understanding in regard to her genius of a son, felt that no good could come for him out of a misalliance with the upper classes.[18]

[18] It could be concluded that Goethe was not in the conventional sense a marrying man. He was happiest either with simple physical sex or with sentimental platonic love: in this period he hovers between the full-blown Lili and the far-off and platonic Auguste von Stolberg – later Frau von Stein will be balanced by vulgar flirtations, later still Christiane by intellectual flirtations, e.g. with Marianne von Willemer.

The decision which he finally took upset his parents even more. At the end of 1774 Goethe was visited by a young Prussian civil servant and man of letters, K. L. von Knebel, who had been engaged as tutor to the young sons of the Dowager Duchess of Sachsen-Weimar. It was the beginning of a friendship which was to last for half a century and it started happily with an invitation from Knebel to go with him to Mainz to meet his pupil, who had come there to meet his bride-to-be, the Princess of Hessen-Darmstadt. Goethe met Klopstock there at the same time and was flattered at receiving an invitation from the young Duke to visit Weimar as his guest. It was a ray of light in a situation becoming emotionally intolerable; Goethe saw too, as his letters show, that here he had the chance (one most other men might ultimately have spoiled) to jump clear into that world of Establishment career-success which had evaded his Werther.

His parents disapproved for the same reasons as they had disapproved of his engagement to Lili. For his self-consciously bourgeois father's 'Roman' virtue, courts were the seats of decadent aristocrats; his son could only be corrupted there. Indeed for the majority of German courts his opinions fitted: fortunately for Goethe, Weimar was an exception. But at first it looked as though Johann Kaspar might be right. The Duke promised Goethe to send a carriage for him; days passed and no carriage arrived. In despair Goethe accepted in 1775 a counter-offer from his father to give him money to travel in Italy (in pre-copyright days successful authorship brought no monetary rewards to equal the fame it won). He set out. But he had only got as far as Heidelberg when news arrived that the Duke's carriage had arrived and was waiting. So he turned back from going south and once more journeyed to the north-east.

Chapter 6

Conquering Hero

When Goethe arrived in Weimar he came as the rising star of German letters. This reputation rested solely on the immediate acclaim which had greeted *Götz* and *Werther*, though it was to be fed during the following years by a few smaller works, notably the rather conventionally written drama *Clavigo*, a not unsuccessful Sturm und Drang version of Lessing's fierce but soberly written social tragedy *Emilia Galotti*, which had just appeared. Despite the acclaim for *Clavigo*, it is significant that the shrewd Merck told Goethe to stop this vein of writing: 'the others can do that sort of thing just as well', he said. His reaction underlines the fact that Goethe was, of course, recognized as a great lyric writer; he was in fact beginning to publish some of his now well-known lyrics.

However, in these last rather feverish and unsatisfactory years in Frankfurt the young man had started a number of different works: since some of them were to become crucial in the canon of his work as a whole, they ought to be at least outlined at this stage of his biography, even if they were not to be completed for decades yet. In one sense Goethe never lived through a more seminal period than these last years in Frankfurt. Of course, he never again really attained a celebrity with the general public comparable to that which he now enjoyed because of *Götz* and *Werther*; indeed, for many readers all over Europe he never was to be anything else except the author of these two. Even today superficial students of European literature find it difficult to name other works by Goethe. The only other one with which Goethe's name is associated so closely is, of course, *Faust*, and the kernel of this dramatic poem too dates back to this period.

It was not only *Faust* which was started during these turbulent years. One other major work was certainly begun now, the drama *Egmont*, about whose genesis we know quite a good deal. We know less about Goethe's second venture into the field of the novel, *Wilhelm Meister*, but it seems likely that the first draft of this work was begun now and very possible that one version of it was even finished before the poet left to take up residence in Weimar. Something similar may be said about the two plays which are most closely associated with his life in Weimar in the late 1770s, *Iphigenie auf Tauris* and *Torquato Tasso*. Though we hear almost nothing of them until the late 1770s, recent research has revealed at least the possibility that the original conception of both dates back to the immediate pre-Weimar years.[19] This would indeed be feasible, for never was there a period when Goethe felt more like a conquering hero, capable of using the world as his oyster, willing to tackle any subject and equipped to treat it with supreme elegance.

Faust is a massive conception about which most educated people have some inkling, even if they have only met it in the sweetened form popularized by Gounod. There is, however, even at the heart of Gounod's pretty-pretty version, a problem which is endemic to the original and its relationship with its author. For Gounod was a serious artist too and his heart was more in devotional music than in 'culinary' opera (as Brecht would have called it), as may be seen in the imposing music he wrote for *Faust*'s final scenes. But the music which has given the opera an inane popularity is the passionate music he wrote for the earlier part of the drama, and notably that connected with Margarete. In this the Frenchman was following in Goethe's footsteps.

For Goethe too has combined at least two plays within one scenario. The 'tragical history' of Dr Faustus came to light in the form of a late Renaissance chap-book, first published at the end of the sixteenth century in Frankfurt, and designed as a 'pop'

[19] H. M. Wolff, *Goethes Weg zur Humanität* (Munich 1951). This is a highly speculative study but, precisely because it has been severely criticized for the most divergent reasons by both Western and Eastern scholars, one wonders whether there may not be a great deal in it. Wolff's case is made with scholarship and care.

satire on the godlessness of the learned classes, to be read by the working-class frequenters of fairs and markets where chap-books were hawked. The dramatic chiaroscuro seized on vivid imaginations; Christopher Marlowe took up this story which was so close to his autobiography. The Marlowe play was brought back to Germany by the wandering English dramatic troupes which played the length and breadth of the Reich during the seventeenth and eighteenth centuries; it never left the repertoire. It sank deep into the life of 'pop' culture, for it was in the form of a child's puppet-theatre that Goethe first encountered it, whilst he seems also to have met it later as a fairground Punch-and-Judy show.

The story was widely known. Goethe may well have seen it as having a personal meaning for himself at the time of his visits to Auerbach's Cellar in Leipzig whilst a student. The Cellar, which is introduced into one of the episodes of the chap-book, maintained its links with Faust through frescoes on its walls. A budding poet might well link these to himself, and re-enact the scenes of academic discontent which were at the heart of the chap-book. It is said too that Goethe could have seen himself as the discontented Faust being bear-led by a sardonic devil in the form of the sophisticated sophomore Behrisch, who initiated the freshman Goethe on his arrival in Leipzig. H. M. Wolff,[20] the modern critic who most favours a Leipzig origin for the drama, points out that the tone of the opening monologue, the famous '*Habe nun, ach . . .*', in which Faust catalogues his criticisms of university study, is that of some of Goethe's letters describing to family and friends his spleen against the elderly Professor Gottsched and the other once great men of the Leipzig Arts Faculty.

Be that as it may, the core of the drama is Goethe's having (like Marlowe) used a chap-book melodrama to canalize intellectual discontent. In the chap-book some (probably clerical) opponent of the universities intended to show that humanistic hubris led wicked scholars to the powers of evil, which doubtless

[20] H. M. Wolff, *Goethe in der Periode der Wahlverwandschaften* (Munich 1952). Here too Wolff plays with speculative reconstructions of known Goethe works, but, again, he uses his imagination only in a way which helps answer questions often left unanswered.

gave them a gay life (enough sex to be titillating and, since it was written for a German reading public, banquets in plenty) – but a short and ultimately damned one. Marlowe concentrated on the tragic situation of the scholar who, although using the powers of evil, still cannot find intellectual satisfaction. Goethe may have intended this to be his theme too, as the opening monologue and the ensuing scene with the Earth Spirit indicate. The Earth Spirit, however, at once introduces a Goethean trademark, appearing neither in the chap-book nor in Marlowe; it flowed naturally, however, from Goethe's early preoccupation with alchemy and the German mystics and cabbalists.

Even Wolff is content to outline the possibility of the tragedy's merely having started in Leipzig, leaving elaboration for the post-Strasbourg years. Here the structure of the whole work could surely have presented itself to the young author. For one thing Goethe had in Strasbourg encountered a real Faust: Herder, as we know from his letters and journal, did consider that he had partaken in vain of all the academic disciplines. His bitter tongue poured out criticisms of contemporary opponents to his constant sick-bed attendant Goethe. He was, moreover, a charismatic figure, courtier and man of the world as well as parson and scholar, and a brilliant talker. He may well have started Goethe on that line of plot-forming which he later, possibly satirically, summarized as 'From Heaven through the world to Hell'. The young lawyer of 1774 had had sufficient cynical contact with the world to design a plot in which an unworldly professor desires rejuvenation, participates in the life outside the university's ivy-clad walls and, disillusioned by the staleness of his experiences (even at the Emperor's court), gladly resigns his soul to the Devil. It is a heaven-storming plot suitable for a young 'genius' and falls indeed into a pattern of similar plays being elaborated in these years, one on Prometheus the fire-bringer (only two acts of it were completed), one on Socrates, one on the Wandering Jew, one on Julius Caesar and one on Mohammed. Goethe was nothing if not ambitious, though there are only outline plots and fragmentary speeches for all these last.

What saved *Faust* from joining the fragments at the bottom of Goethe's drawer was a chance happening in the Frankfurt

Law Courts at the start of his frequenting them. A maidservant was brought up and condemned to death for infanticide. There was nothing very unusual about either the case or the sentence. But the inhumanity of such penal legislation became, for the Sturm und Drang lawyer looking on, a symbol of all kinds of things which were teasing his mind. At the most open level, the level of public life, the radical Goethe saw the sentence as a mark of the oppressive society crushing an innocent victim who scarcely knew what it was she had done. Not only had the girl been cruelly punished with all the majesty of a state pageant, the young radical saw in the hypocrisy of his society's morality a condemnation of the whole class system. For he had seen in Leipzig and Strasbourg (and doubtless in his home town too) that members of the upper classes felt it part of their natural way of life to seduce any girl who came across their path, and especially girls from the lower classes.[21] How bitterly young radical students regarded the double morality of their ruling class is to be seen in the fact that all the major dramatists of the Sturm und Drang movement chose a similar theme for a dramatic poem: Lenz in his *Soldaten* showed an officer seducing the daughter of a draper; Wagner in his *Die Kindermörderin* made his innocent victim the daughter of a butcher; Schiller's Luise in *Kabale und Liebe* was the daughter of a lowly court musician.

Each of the dramatists took a different aspect of the seduction motive as his crux. What was common to them was the manner in which they laid bare the way in which such immorality was regarded as normal for the upper classes; the innocent victim highlighted a cosy and essentially healthy bourgeois home life. It was the nearest approach to a literary treatment in Germany of the kind of moral freedom for the middle classes which was demanded in the West by Tom Paine and Rousseau. Only a few individualists like Daniel Schubart or G. A. Bürger dared to

[21] Surprisingly little has been written on the subject of the defence of middle-class sexual morals as a major theme in the Sturm und Drang period. I have summarized the evidence in an article, 'Death the Defender of Honour', *Philologica Pragensia*, Vol. xii, No. 1 (1969). The subject is also touched on by Braemer in the earlier part of the work cited in n. 5 (*Goethes Prometheus . . .*).

make direct political attacks on the German *ancien régime*; possibly none of the other young men were even aware of the link between individual immorality and the political system of their homeland. There is a final scene in Lenz's tragedy in which two aristocratic characters meditate on the horrors they have witnessed; their reflections are as shallow as their suggested remedies are absurd. Obviously Lenz was no Diderot. Nor was Goethe, as the idealized politics of *Götz* had already shown.

But the treatment of infanticide in this way was none the less a radical political step. Goethe was driven to think about the serving-wench for another reason. We do not know if he seduced Friederike or even kissed Lotte. But it is certain that he felt guilty about his relations with both girls. Just as he had associated his feelings at leaving Lotte with the suicide of Jerusalem, so now he associated his feelings at leaving Friederike and Lotte with the presumed feelings of the faithless seducer who had left the Frankfurt serving-wench in the lurch. It is not even likely that the seducer was other than an apprentice, a youth of her own class. But for Goethe the idea of class intruded itself immediately, as it had done in *Werther* when he considered the whole background of society which drove his hero to take his own life – snobbery and love were indistinguishably intertwined. They were so impossible to disentangle that Goethe soon forgot what it was that had originally caught his attention in the lawsuit. Gretchen became a figure in the Faust story. The dissatisfied academic in the sixteenth-century chap-book had been proffered sixteenth-century sex and had enjoyed it in the form of the sex symbol best known to the contemporary reading public, Helen of Troy, with whom, says the original, he lived for many years and begat a son. There was no more titillation in it than that. Goethe went more deeply into the possibilities opened up by this archetypal situation.

His Faust was now to become the seducer not of a demigoddess but of a petty-bourgeois girl, the shatterer of a cosy domesticity. There are many hints in the *Urfaust*, the manuscript which was written at this period, of what this was to entail. Above all it led to Gretchen's deceiving her family (a device which makes her accidentally kill her mother with an overdose of sleeping-draught), conniving with a lecherous neighbour who plays bawd, and finally bringing disaster on her honest brother who seeks to avenge her honour by challenging the supernatural seducer. Once the opportunities became clear to the young poet, the original thread of intention snapped again and again. The original seduction scene was retained, but at once (possibly following a lead from Lessing's treatment of his own seduced heroine in *Emilia Galotti*) Goethe inserted a scene showing Gretchen's own internal moral struggle, which introduced an already composed ballad whose eeriness perfectly catches the tone of the play – so perfectly that Goethe went on to use set-piece poems (not only ballads) to underline emotional moments of the action, a device he continued to use in *Egmont* and *Iphigenie*. Faust was introduced into Gretchen's home by his familiar – and at once what was devised as sexual titillation became one of the most lyrical scenes in the drama, Faust being borne aloft by his admiration for this blissful domesticity. For all the young Goethe's titanism, there was a strongly bourgeois streak in his make-up, and, from the days when he had learned to draw Chardin-like interiors with the allegedly classicist painter Oeser in Leipzig, he was brought back to domesticity again and again.

It was necessary now for the dramatist to describe the way in which the Devil brought about Gretchen's seduction. This involved the introduction of the bawd. One of the strangest things about Goethe's Devil, Mephistopheles (a mere name in the chap-book, a pallid figure from the mystery-plays in Marlowe), is that he is such a likeable fellow. This was indeed Goethe's addition to the legend – though it was a fairly normal device in the mystery-plays to make the Devil the humorist, a tradition which was maintained amongst the wandering troupes. But Goethe's devil was no simple knockabout comedian. We have already noted that he may have used the figure of a blasé Leipzig fellow-student when dealing with the theme in his presumed Leipzig plot. This plot was notably concerned with criticism of the academic curriculum, a subject about which sophisticated sophomores are usually as eloquent as they are brilliant.

The Behrisch Mephistopheles from Leipzig was now put into the foundry again and mixed with a new figure of cynicism,

Merck, editor of the spiky literary magazine for which Goethe was working. Merck has many claims on our attention in this respect. Though only a civil servant in the small state of Hessen-Darmstadt, he was the intellectual leader of the court intelligentsia and their acknowledged *maître de plaisirs*. As such, he invented all kinds of satirical and boisterous diversions, some of which caused no little scandal amongst the sober-sided citizens of the duchy's towns. The gilded young of this Sturm und Drang period *were* notably active and boisterous, as we know from Goethe's first few years with Duke Karl August in Weimar. But under his frivolous exterior, Merck was a serious thinker, and was later to support the revolutionary side in France to the point where the Wars of Intervention caused his suicide. To add weight to the equation of Merck and Mephistopheles, one may note that his portrait shows a genial but saturnine dolichocephalic head with heavily-marked eyebrows capable of being raised to greatly 'cynical' effect.

No doubt the fragments of academic criticism which mark Mephistopheles' arrival in the *Urfaust* go back to Behrisch; the boisterous Mephistopheles who invents the stratagem for introducing Faust to the bawd and through her to Gretchen may plausibly be related to Merck. This devil is much more a cynical man of the world than one of the powers of evil. Indeed some critics, notably Karl Jaspers,[22] complained that Goethe had no real sense of radical evil. This is arguable; what is certain is that he sensed the shocking moral dilemma in which his situation placed the hero. Of all the *Urfaust* scenes (and they included only the important dramatic ones – the young poet left out all the difficult transitional scenes, such as those in which Faust might have first met his familiar, and also those which might have explained why he deserted his seduced victim) perhaps the most powerful was the one in which Faust might have, learning that Gretchen was in prison and had been condemned for the murder of their illegitimate child, turned on Mephistopheles and berated him. The sole reply was the chilling 'Did we force ourselves on you or you on us?' No more dramatic statement of the

[22] K. Jaspers, *Unsere Zukunft und Goethe* (Stuttgart 1948).

existential dilemma of Man can be imagined: this is the only answer to Jaspers that is needed. Man does indeed make his own evil.

Having got so far, however, Goethe had long since left behind the idea that the Gretchen tragedy was merely a gloss on contemporary conditions in Germany. His absorption into the poetic detail of his creation is perhaps best observed in the *Urfaust* scenes devoted to Gretchen. The slight sketches which point to her realization of her predicament and the incredibly powerful scene of her self-castigation in the cathedral not only show Goethe's sense of the full scope of radical evil; they are also the best answer to those modern critics who have denied that Goethe was really a writer of Tragedy. Doubtless Goethe was unable – because unwilling – to write neat paradigmatic tragedy on the lines of the Greeks or their imitators in the reign of Louis XIV and Louis XV. There are other forms of writing for the tragic stage, however, and it was these that Goethe developed, not only in *Faust* but later in *Iphigenie*, *Tasso*, and *Die natürliche Tochter*.

Goethe may have had from the outset ideas about a complete drama based on the chap-book and/or Marlowe. We have no evidence of this for another decade. When he came to finish his earlier fragment in the early 1790s he realized that there was more than sufficient in the germ of *Urfaust* to make a complete dramatic offering, and he filled out the early skeleton, calling the final product Part One. Many years later, at the very end of his long life, he was to distil the experience of eight decades into a schematic plot based on the original legend and his own additions to it, which he called Part Two. This was a different drama, and it was certainly written in a very different way.

The author of the *Urfaust* left his fragment, dissatisfied probably at the difficulties he could see in motivating the disparate parts which he had now gathered together. He turned to another Faust-like subject, one just as remarkable in its way, though without the intellectual overtones of the chap-book. This other subject was *Egmont*. Much more of this play was written in Frankfurt than of *Faust*, but *Egmont* too had to wait, for its polishing, until the turbulence of the Frankfurt years had settled with the poet's new life in Weimar.

What attracted Goethe to the subject of the revolt of the Netherlands also throws light on the Sturm und Drang lawyer's political outlook. Indeed, in order to do the subject justice one should bear in mind – something which it is difficult to do today – that actually in 1774 the Revolt of the Netherlands was one of the paradigmatic revolutions for young radicals. True, the Americans had begun their War of Independence against the British, but contemporary wars and revolts do not possess the same poetic fascination for onlooking students as those safely in the past. The English Civil War might have been considered exemplary by some, but the Continent has always experienced difficulty in seeing Cromwell as a glamorous figure (Victor Hugo is one of the few foreign dramatists to have considered him worthy of hero-worship). In order to look back to what eighteenth-century thinkers felt to be situations comparable to their own, it was necessary to go back either to the struggle of the Netherlanders against Spain or to various episodes in German history, which (as *Götz* shows) were none of them easy to present in the straightforward black-and-white fashion demanded by the theatre. It will be noted that the historian Schiller was to pursue this same intellectual path, beginning with a detailed study of the Revolt of the Netherlands and continuing with a study of the Thirty Years War so subtle that it is still usable for the historian wishing to study this period.

However for Goethe it was not so much the period which was fascinating as one idea. *Götz* (whose story Goethe manipulated wildly in the interests of achieving an exciting plot) had ended with the word 'Freedom', the guiding light of the eponymous hero's life, breathed by him on his bitter deathbed; *Egmont* takes up the theme and makes it the core of another plot, centred almost to the point of obsessiveness on this one point. The story of the new tragedy is not so much the story of the political fight of an oppressed people against reaction, as the story of one leader-figure obsessed to the point of recklessness with the concept of freedom. In order to pay such homage to the idea of freedom, Goethe had, in fact, to do a great deal of violence to the historical facts concerning the real Count Egmond who was executed in the mid-sixteenth century for conspiracy against Philip II of

Spain. The real Egmond was indeed a leader of his people in their revolt but he was also a man in late middle age, married and with a large family. Goethe could not imagine the hero he wanted with such disqualifications, so he made his hero at least *seem* youthful, and relieved him of wife and children. To compensate for this, however, he showed him fighting for freedom in yet another sphere. With the figure of Gretchen Goethe had sublimated the sex-war aspect of Sturm und Drang dramatic thinking into a poem of misunderstandings between poor girl and socially superior lover; in *Egmont* Goethe was to treat the social conventions of sex with sublime disdain. Klärchen, his hero's mistress, is as petty-bourgeois as Gretchen; but at no stage did the author imply that her relations with Egmont had any respectable future in *this* world. Yet Egmont himself is so noble that the feeling of *noblesse oblige* is one of the elements of his downfall: he cannot bring himself to believe that anyone as open as himself can be treated by anyone, even the wicked Spanish viceroy Alba, as a conspirator, and arrested and condemned without public trial.

It is indeed this superb recklessness which fascinated Goethe about his hero. It is difficult at this remove to discover from what source (if any) he drew his picture of a (most un-Dutch) character of this kind. The fact is that he needed at this period of his life, when he was juggling in his mind with Mohammed and Ahasuerus and Caesar, to think in terms of superhuman figures. Egmont came as close to being a superhuman figure as the poet could make him without flying overtly in the face of credibility: the most effective speeches in the play are those in which the hero expresses belief in his own charisma. Grudging modern critics may see logical flaws in the superb apotheosis of freedom with which the play ends. It was, in fact, not intended by its author to be treated as a sermon; it was planned as a rhapsody, almost literally as music. The play gives detailed instructions for the staging of the final balletic movements of the action, 'melodrama' of this kind being a normal eighteenth-century stage custom, and it was fitting that Beethoven should have been inspired by Goethe to write for it some of his most exciting music. It was typical of the confusions of the times, however, that

Goethe, whose tastes in music had been formed in Leipzig, should not have approved. Mozart was his favourite composer, and Romantic modernism could only touch him when he later met it in the elegant music of the young Mendelssohn.

Fortunately Goethe was later impelled to work over the drama and give it more coherence. The critics of Goethe's optimism gain strength from the fact that the final part to be written in the 1780s was the fourth act, which introduces the figure of Egmont's opponent and conqueror, the evil Duke of Alba. In the early version this must have been very wild; in the later version the poet toned it down. Truth to tell, Goethe was simply not interested in presenting Alba: obviously evil exists in the world, or the good men (like Egmont) would inevitably win all along the line. As it is, experience shows how often the best end sadly; hence (Goethe implies) it can be taken for granted that there is an evil Fate which will eventually get the better of the Egmonts of this world. Goethe's mind was bent on analysing and presenting what makes the Egmonts function. He worked out a series of crowd-scenes from Belgian folk-life, which gave him more pleasure than his descriptions of the Spaniards, and which were based on the Shakespearian techniques he had imbibed at Herder's side. But whereas the 'pop' scenes were riotously undisciplined in *Götz*, in the *Egmont* crowd-scenes there is a rhythm and an order which is as controlled as the comparable sequence of ballads and poems sung by Klärchen, or the poems and songs of Gretchen. The first folk-scene starts the play and mirrors Egmont's charisma; the second shows the plot thickening and mirrors growing dissension; the third shows the cowed Flemings against the lightning of Klärchen's tragic resolve to die for her lover. Of the other works written in this period it will perhaps be more appropriate to deal with *Iphigenie* and *Tasso* in connection with Weimar, where they largely belong. Suffice it at this point to say that *Iphigenie* involves a relationship between brother and sister so strong as to be almost incestuous, whilst *Tasso* concerns a series of love-hate relationships between a very tightly-knit group of individuals whose influence both encourages and frustrates the development of a poet's individuality. Goethe was not sufficiently experienced for either plot at this time and so they had to wait another decade. But the kernel of the relationship between Iphigenia and Orestes, outlined for all time by Aeschylus, could very easily have been taken up by Goethe if his feelings towards his sister Cornelia were as unusually warm as was suggested by Barker Fairley in his psychoanalytical study of the young Goethe.[23] Whether they were or were not, it is certain that the young man did feel very strongly about her in his early years in Weimar, when she, who had been one of his closest confidantes, suddenly fell in love and married, leaving Frankfurt for good. Since Goethe was being bombarded from all sides by news of his friends marrying (notably Herder, Lotte and Lili), the question of such relationships may well have come largely to the fore in his mind.

As to the problem of the poet in society, this is one which faces all young men of genius. Tasso's problem, the question of how the bourgeois poet is to behave in an aristocratic society to which he is socially inferior, had just begun to intrude itself on Goethe, as he mixed with the socially superior society surrounding his fiancée Lili Schönemann. Lili was also a spoiled 'deb' from the very top stratum of the moneyed Frankfurt nobility, yet despite their different social backgrounds they seem at first to have got on very well with each other; the cooling off of the relationship had little to do with the social disparity which so worried Goethe's mother (after all, Goethe was only to escape Lili's world by running away to an even remoter and less approved one, the ducal court of Weimar). In fact, Lili, for all her frivolous pleasure-seeking, was also a good bourgeois product, as her future behaviour was to show: she guided her wealthy and aristocratic husband safely through many of the vicissitudes caused by the French Wars. Asked at the end of his life which of all his girl-friends he now thought might really have made him lastingly happy, Goethe unhesitatingly replied 'Lili', which may or may not be significant. One suspects indeed that the real problem about what the poet called Lili's 'menagerie' was not the proprietress but the other animals, just as in *Tasso* the main

[23] B. Fairley, *A Study of Goethe* (Oxford 1969). Although this one of the best modern works on the poet, psycho-analytical approach is also very speculative.

problem is not the Duke of Ferrara and his lovely sister, but the jealous rivalry of Tasso's hated and loved colleague, the Prime Minister Antonio. Goethe could not yet fully appreciate the problem of Tasso and the princess; but he was surrounded on all sides by the questions of conduct which affect a man of acknowledged genius living in a world where his position is for most people of only doubtful validity.

This problem so affected Goethe that he treated it at length in his second venture into the form of the novel. *Wilhelm Meister* was to become one of the models for the development of the modern German novel and especially of that most important branch known as the *Bildungsroman*, the novel showing the mental growth and development of a central character.[24] But it undoubtedly started in the poet's last years at home as a purely personal expression of dissatisfaction with his own personal and social position. The young hero (originally thought of not as William the Master but as William the Apprentice or even as William the Pupil) was a young man from a middle-class background, bored by the mercantile atmosphere, and devoted to the thought of escaping into creative writing. In the conditions of the eighteenth century there are two main avenues open to him, poetry or drama, and he opts, through a series of interesting *rencontres* which are to become major themes in the novel as it develops, for the latter. He leaves his home, not after a violent quarrel but in a gentle breaking-away movement utterly reminiscent of the young Goethe, and falls in with a series of theatrical people who have a great influence on his life. His crucial experience is not to be in the theatre, however, but in an aristocratic castle to which the wandering troupe with whom Wilhelm is associated is invited. It is here that Wilhelm encounters another Mephisto-figure, Jarno, a gentleman deeply permeated by the cult of Shakespeare: Jarno-Herder wins Wilhelm to this allegiance.

There are many other streams running through this large work. In the Frankfurt version, as critics surmise it today, they

[24] See M. Gerhard, *Der deutsche Entwicklungsroman bis zu Goethes Wilhelm Meister* (Halle 1926).

were rudimentary.[25] In the early 1780s Goethe reworked this version and expanded it somewhat, the result being an equally unfinished novel, the manuscript of which was only re-discovered in 1910. It was not until the 1790s that a final version was to be written and this is the fully fashioned product which stands at the head of modern German prose-writing. Its roots, however, lie in a mirroring by the poet of his final discontents in his home town. *Wilhelm Meister's Mission in the Theatre* (the title of the completed second version) was also Goethe's feeling of mission in art. It was now to take him to Weimar.

[25] Wolff, op. cit. (n. 19). The literature on *Faust* is, of course, enormous. There is a good summary of literature up to the time of writing in E. C. Mason, *Goethe's Faust* (Oxford 1970). Some other works are mentioned in the solid *Faust: Interpretation* (Oxford 1957), by A. Gillies.

Chapter 7

Settling into Weimar

Goethe spent the first year in Weimar gaining the confidence and, over and above this, the intimate friendship of Duke Karl August. It was a remarkable thing, this friendship between the young aristocrat and the rising poet. One tends to take it for granted but there was a lot in its way. The average young German aristocrat of the time was the wealthy Guards officer type, good on a horse and with guns, sufficiently acquainted with the *grand monde* to be able to hold his own at an official reception and, in most cases, able (and willing) to make polite conversation with ladies of his own class and to flirt (often outrageously) with women of lower classes. A great many of the young aristocrats in Karl August's position were completely corrupted by their absolute power and placed no rein on their sensual appetites at all: they were immoderate in every vice from sloth and greed (for money, food and drink) to outrageous sensuality and violence. Despite which, one must say, the cultural tradition, implanted by certain of the Italian Renaissance courts and magnified, above all, at Versailles and St James's, did take root in some of the smaller German courts, the lead coming partly from the Imperial court at Vienna and partly from the Potsdam of the Hohenzollerns, where Frederick II was beginning to devote a good deal of time to cultural and artistic pursuits.

There had long been a cultural tradition in Weimar: Bach had made music there, and various Renaissance painters had stayed there at times. This tradition was reinforced when the father of Karl August married a princess from the house of Braunschweig-Wolfenbüttel, for the northern house not only patronized the Arts but took an active part in the fostering of a native German culture. When the Duchess, Anna Amalia, was left a widow with two teenage sons on her hands, she therefore set about finding them the best tutor her income could buy. She chose first Wieland, who was a good showman and had just written his *Der Goldene Spiegel*, a 'mirror for kings' with which he had hoped to gain a foothold in the Imperial court. But Vienna considered the erotic writings of Wieland's youth a disqualification for its highly Catholic atmosphere and Austrian *philosophes* feared serious competition from outside their own ranks. A writer like Sonnenfels today seems provincial, and he was provincial; but he happened to be at the levers of power and could stop better men from coming near them. In Weimar there was not this jealousy. It appeared only in what could well have been simply a form of snobbery when, in 1776, Karl August suggested that Goethe became a member of his Privy Council (which was really the Cabinet of his tiny state): then the chairman, a baron of the noble local family of von Fritsch, carried his objections to the point of offering his resignation. Karl August smoothed his ruffled feelings and Goethe thus placed his foot on the first rung of the ladder which was to lead him to fame and honours. This was just what Goethe-Werther needed to lead him out of his Ossianic melancholy and restlessness.

Wieland had undoubtedly helped sophisticate the young heir apparent, who, because of his father's death, became reigning duke at the age of eighteen. But he proved a hopeless teacher and Anna Amalia had to engage yet another tutor for actual didactic purposes. This was a young Prussian called von Knebel who was good at his job and should also be given credit for having created the tastes of the young man who was to become Goethe's bosom friend. There were, of course, some social difficulties; at times Goethe's 'Bohemian' manners (possibly encouraged by his lack of restraint in Weimar) caused him to be snubbed when visiting the other courts with his lord and master; friend Lenz, moreover, soon followed Goethe to the court and caused a mysterious scandal (some have said he actually dared to try to snatch a kiss from Karl August's young wife); from time to time Karl August's aristocratic attitude to sex was to cause his friend difficulties, notably when the Duke took up with actresses from

Goethe's company – it was as a result of a quarrel with one of these that Goethe finally resigned his manager's post at the court theatre. Goethe was to have trouble too with Karl August's adventures into the military life: the Duke became a Prussian major-general during his absence in Italy.

Indeed there must have been good reasons for Goethe to tell Eckermann at the end of his life that he had really never had a day of cloudless peace. One cannot doubt that Goethe, too, must soon have discovered the difficulties that made Wieland write to Lavater in 1776 (after only three years in Weimar):

> Goethe will probably be staying here for a long time – he is mightily taken with everything and is now setting out on the adventure from which I drew back as soon as I saw that it was being kept for another. Oh Lavater, Lavater! how lucky for you that you have never had to get to know the *grand monde*, the children of princes, the courtiers, the majordomos and so on, from such a close range and at such cost as I have had to do!

Indeed the extent of Goethe's involvement in Weimar should never be exaggerated to the point where one cannot explain to oneself at the same time the frustrations which finally made him, after ten years, suddenly drop everything and, without asking royal permission, steal away to Italy and stay there for a couple of years, to re-emerge as a full-time writer. Weight of business and an unsatisfactory love-affair are only two of the other pressures which were operating on him. Basically life at court was difficult for one who was not only a poet but, and essentially, from a lower social class. Goethe makes light of the patent of nobility which Karl August obtained for him in 1782; this was actually as essential for his peace of mind as obtaining a place for his son in the royal service was to be later.

In the first years in Weimar Goethe spent the greater part of his time sharing Karl August's aristocratic pleasures: it is even reported that they would spend hours on end simply standing in the market-place of Weimar cracking their long riding-whips. In addition there was riding and hunting, and Goethe taught the court the delights of skating. There were 'orgies' with country girls and gypsies, but, in fact, Karl August did not belong to the sex-mad type of upper-class youth. Goethe, too, soon ceased to be interested in casual affairs as he fell violently in love with a court lady, Charlotte von Stein, wife of the Duke's Master of Horse. Baron von Stein was a bluff squire who had little in common with his delicate and sentimental lady-wife; he spent most of his time away from their town house, living in the country. Such an arrangement was by no means unusual amongst the aristocracy; the purpose of the marriage had been fulfilled with the birth of a string of children, three of whom were still living at this time. Frau von Stein was six years older than Goethe and in many ways a typical provincial blue-stocking. But she was on the spot; she was the first lady of breeding with whom Goethe had been on intimate terms – and she was sufficient to inspire Germany's greatest lyric poet to produce gushing rivers of wonderful verse. He had needed an ideal woman ever since the days when he had invented Gretchen.

Naturally the affair had to be pursued with some secrecy, but distances were not great in the tiny walled city and Goethe had been given, almost as soon as he arrived in Weimar, a little cottage on the outskirts of the town, overlooking a poetically 'wild' stretch of the Ilm rivulet. Here he settled down to a bachelor existence which enabled him to come and go as he wished, spend nights gazing at moon and river, and awake to write down his poetry as it flooded in on him. Moreover, just as he gained the love of the royal pair through his assiduity in inventing new pleasures for them, so he made himself a needed part of the Stein household by taking in hand the education of the oldest boy, Fritz, then aged eleven. For a time the boy even lived in the garden-house with Goethe and his Frankfurt manservant. For Fritz, too, Goethe undertook in 1783 a second journey to the Harz Mountains (further north than Weimar). This was to have a great effect on the poet himself. The first Harz trip had been in the winter of 1777: Goethe's first post on the Privy Council was to act as Commissioner of Mines. The Harz was one of Germany's major mining areas and so a trip there was likely to be fruitful for the new bureaucrat. Goethe took Karl August, and the small party combined walking, riding, hunting, shooting – and studying mining and mineralogy. Six years later the poet's mining interest had become a passionate devotion to geology and other earth-sciences, and the journey with Fritz von Stein thus served an educational purpose for both participants.

But it was a poet who was undertaking all these adventures. The wild scenery of the Harz, so different from the lush pastures of Thuringia and the luxuriance of the Main valley, made its impact on Goethe. On both his early trips (he was to make two more in the course of the years after his Italian journey) he climbed the Brocken, the legendary site of devilish revels on Midsummer night. Once again a thread was spun which was to keep alive his interest in the Faust story, and especially the background of Mephistopheles.

Goethe's life in Weimar was filled with activity. To his mining commitment he soon added other posts, until finally he was acting as *de facto* Prime Minister of the little duchy. It was undoubtedly too much work for a poet and after his return from Italy Goethe gave up most of the purely civil service offices. But he continued with the post of unofficial *maître de plaisirs* to the court. From the start this had been his favourite role. Almost the only works larger than lyric poems which stemmed from these years were occasional playlets, masques and comedies intended to be performed by the court (Wieland, too, participated in these activities: the older poet had long since abandoned his early attachment to the drama, but he too was harnessed to the provision of playlets for the amateur theatre).[26]

By inviting Wieland to Weimar, Anna Amalia had laid the foundation for the duchy's growth into the cultural capital of Germany. After Wieland came Goethe, and the latter too now brought new talent to the court. At the end of 1775 he had already suggested to Herder that he should accept the post of head of the Lutheran Church in the duchy, and shortly afterwards the Herder family, too, was living in the town. Herder was not one of the prototypes of Mephistopheles for nothing; he

[26] G. Sichardt, *Das Weimarer Liebhabertheater unter Goethes Leitung* (Weimar 1957).

was a difficult person to deal with and relations between him and Goethe were often strained. But three of Germany's brightest stars were now united in one social ambience. With time, of course, the constellation was to expand. Schiller was to come in the 1790s and later a less high-powered but still important team of younger men of science and learning; famous professors at the university of Jena (Weimar's state university), such as Fichte, Oken and D'Alton; Heinrich Meyer, a Swiss artist and art historian who became the first director of the art school Goethe was instrumental in founding; and Frédéric Soret, a young Genevan patrician and scientist, who came as tutor to the royal children (he was the nephew of the great Genevan scientist-politician Dumont and was to put Goethe in touch with the French Romantics from Delacroix and David d'Angers to Ampère and the early Saint-Simonians).

Undoubtedly the most important literary aspect of Goethe's first decade in Weimar was the great outpouring of lyric poetry which was occasioned above all by his love for Frau von Stein. This was a very important part of the young poet's life but it caused him pain as well as joy. For in addition to the need to keep the depth of the affair secret, there was the undoubted fact that the lady was by no means Goethe's intellectual equal and caused him much mental strife. If we are to judge by Frau von Stein's behaviour after the end of the affair, she was, in fact, very limited in outlook. Goethe must have become aware of this, even though he continued to write her passionate letters during the Italian tour : it was not until he returned to Weimar that the break became final, Frau von Stein letting him see, from the very first days of his return, that she was deeply offended by the secrecy with which her worshipper had torn himself away from her whilst allegedly on summer holiday at Karlsbad (in the Czech northern mountains, a fashionable summer *villeggiatura* for the European aristocracy).

From Italy Goethe wrote to the Duke that he had felt both deep disquiet about his life in Weimar and also a need to live unrestrictedly amongst works of art. This reawakening of the feeling that he must above all be an artist had been growing towards the end of the first decade in Weimar. It had doubtless been nourished by the two major tours of these years, both undertaken in company with the Duke: in the spring of 1778 a visit to Berlin, where the outward signs of the War of the Bavarian Succession stirred in him a feeling of great events in the making; and at the end of 1779 an extended tour down the Rhine to French and German Switzerland (which had even taken him to the verge of the St Gotthard Pass). There were shorter visits to other courts which undoubtedly impressed him with their artistic culture and simultaneously made him feel aware of the creative time he himself was wasting.

Goethe travelled rapidly down to Italy under the incognito of a writer and painter and was soon lost amongst the large colony of German artists and literary men assembled in Rome. He became intimate with the very best of these, notably the painters Tischbein, Hackert and Angelika Kaufmann. He also befriended yet another self-made intellectual in the person of the parson K. P. Moritz, whose interest in the Classics was to stand Goethe in good stead during the next decade as he moved more and more towards a revived interest in Classical metres.

All kinds of new interests crowded in on him in Italy. Or rather, many new experiences filled out gaps in his knowledge of fields in which he had earlier begun to interest himself only theoretically. While it is interesting to note how he ignored the monuments of medieval and Gothic Italy, it is also significant that he was not terribly impressed by the sight of the Greek temple at Paestum. His artistic taste developed more and more in the direction of Palladian rococo – to the point where his return visit to Italy in 1790 led to an almost complete disillusionment with the country. Italy in fact served a psychological purpose, offering him colour and liveliness at a moment when his genius was being stifled by a too catholic immersion into the life of a small provincial German court. In Italy the teeming life of an uninhibited people made its mark on him. There is undoubtedly, too, more than simple guesswork behind Barker Fairley's suggestion that Goethe had his first sexual experience towards the end of his stay, when he lived for a brief period with a light-hearted Milanese girl, Maddalena Riggi. This experience undoubtedly paved the way for his astonishingly frank relationship with

Christiane Vulpius, which was entered into in 1790, almost immediately after the return from Italy.

Almost more important than his actual experience of the pullulating Italian scene, however, was the way in which the luxuriant flora of Italy stimulated his scientific interests, in morphology in general and botany in particular. This philosophical rebirth at last set free his creative faculties and he took up again all kinds of unfinished works which had travelled with him in his luggage to Italy. Not only did he revise *Egmont* but he wrote two significant scenes for *Faust*, beginning the painful process of motivating the impressionistic sketches of the first draft. One of these scenes is, strangely enough, the Witches' Kitchen, preoccupation with this weird Nordic episode showing the intellectual ferment bubbling within his brain. The intellectual strain is documented too in the work now carried out on *Iphigenie* and, above all, *Tasso*.

Despite the poet's keenness to observe his incognito (this was difficult because he was, after all, a widely known literary figure and also a not unimportant politician), he continued to keep up his connections with the court of Weimar and finally in 1788 he felt that he had had his fill of rejuvenation and could safely return home. It is perhaps the most significant aspect of this whole decade that home for Goethe now meant Weimar. At no stage was there now any serious consideration of a move elsewhere (as, at a later stage, we know to have been the case with both Herder and Schiller). Weimar had gained its most famous inhabitant for good. The Italian journey had been merely an interruption; it was never intended to be a final separation. The middle-class youth with no prospects save in the Law had become a Weimar courtier with an imposing town house of his own. Shortly after his return from Italy the house was to welcome a mistress, too.

Chapter 8

The Poet and the Revolution

It is difficult to over-estimate how rash Goethe was in taking the young Christiane Vulpius, who in 1788 became his mistress, to live in his house. One can only explain his action as the deed of a man who realized that he was the most celebrated intellectual in the whole of the German Reich. Mistresses were not uncommon amongst the aristocracy (and Goethe was now a member of that class), but even in such circles the presence of a mistress living in a man's house was normally regarded as a mark of open depravity. Moreover, Weimar was a small and not particularly immoral royal residency, so that an action like Goethe's gave rise to a great deal of unfavourable gossip. Goethe took not only Christiane to live with him but her mother as well.

The gossip might have been less venomous had Christiane been a strikingly lovely or talented young girl but, except in Goethe's eyes, she was not. She was a pleasant, somewhat fleshy blonde with curly hair; and, a fact which particularly harmed her in the world's eyes, she had no education. At the time when Goethe made her acquaintance she was a factory-girl, working in a small local workshop which manufactured paper flowers run by Weimar's one capitalist, F. J. Bertuch.[27] The immediate occasion of their meeting was her need to beg of Goethe a favour for her brother. This young man was later to fulfil the promise of his intellectual aspirations; at this stage they caused him to put

[27] W. H. Bruford, *Culture and Society in Classical Weimar 1775–1806* (Cambridge 1962). I should say how much all younger English scholars stand in Prof. Bruford's debt, not only to this work but, in our youth, to his still unmatched *Germany in the 18th century* (Cambridge 1935, reprinted 1965).

forward his sister to ask Goethe to give him employment in the state library. Later he became a good librarian and, above all, he dabbled in writing, achieving with his adventure-story, *Rinaldo Rinaldini*, what may be called the first popular success for a lowbrow novel in the nineteenth century.

Goethe's sensuality had undoubtedly been awakened by his adventures in Italy and he soon seduced Christiane. But he then fell deeply in love with her, particularly when she bore him a son. Yet despite his love and despite the gossip attendant on his strange way of living, he did not make up his mind to marry her until 1806, after an untoward episode during the French occupation. Drunken French soldiers insulted Christiane, but she held them at bay and prevented them from invading the house (which might have led to an assault on Goethe – Lavater was killed by marauding French soldiers in Zürich in the same period). Goethe clearly preferred to overlook the malicious remarks about his way of life rather than suffer even more barbed comment for having married a woman who, judging from almost all contemporary description save that of his open-minded and deeply percipient mother, looked her class and never succeeded in behaving in anything but a motherly and thoroughly bourgeois fashion. The devotion with which Christiane nursed him in his serious illnesses may also have eventually overcome his other doubts as to the wisdom of marrying her.

The hostility with which Christiane's arrival was greeted by Frau von Stein can be imagined – the breach with Goethe was not healed until Goethe's serious illness of 1801. The feeling spread throughout the duchy and there were few houses of any note in which Goethe and his *de facto* wife were received. Not even Schiller, who became from 1794 until his death in 1805 the closest of intellectual collaborators with Goethe, could prevail on his own (rather aristocratic) wife to receive Christiane, although Goethe was an almost constant visitor to their home, both before the Schillers moved to Weimar and after.

One can only ascribe Goethe's behaviour to sublime belief in his star. Occasional fits of resentment may have been worked off in close human contact with the Weimar theatrical circle, whose Director Goethe became in 1791 and whom he entertained in a very hearty fashion. That Goethe was oblivious to the feelings of the outside world is unlikely; the hurt he received may well have been responsible for the deterioration in health that ultimately led to the bronchial illness of 1801 which nearly killed him. He was left with a hypochondria which pursued him on and off for the rest of his life, long though this was to be. Disappointment may also have contributed to making him haughty towards strangers and in large gatherings.

Doubtless his health was not improved by the bouts of military campaigning which also marked this period. Whilst the poet was in Italy, Karl August, returning gratefully to one of the more normal occupations open to royalty, had become a general in the armed forces of Prussia. This led him to take his erring minister to Silesia with him almost as soon as he had returned from Italy and then, in the 1790s, on a series of campaigns connected with the more or less unsuccessful opposition of the German princes to the French revolutionary governments. The Valmy campaign in particular was fought under distressing climatic conditions. Goethe not only had the opportunity cold-bloodedly to test his composure under fire (just as he had cured his earlier aversion to heights by constantly ascending the tower of Strasbourg Cathedral); he also had to test his diplomacy during a visit to the revolutionary intellectuals governing Mainz, and his physical fortitude during the siege which ultimately brought counter-revolutionary order back to the town.

It was a strenuous period. The outbreak of the Revolution gave the German intellectuals considerable mental exercise which was not always pleasant.[28] At first almost all of them favoured a turn of events which seemed so fittingly to crown the efforts at intellectual liberation made by the French *philosophes* throughout the century. But it was one thing to approve in theory what at first seemed merely to be a putting into practice of the ideals of Rousseau, Paine and the American War of Independence, and another to see – as it appeared – this new-found freedom degenerating into scruffy internecine warfare amongst the revolutionaries and, finally, into the Reign of Terror directed

[28] The best treatment of the period is still G. P. Gooch, *Germany and the French Revolution* (F. Cass 1965).

against the royal family and the court. It should be noted, too, that Koblenz became the seat of the most intransigent *émigrés* and kept up a constant stream of hostile counter-revolutionary propaganda, not without effect in the German courts, which had little to gain and obviously much to lose if the French infection spread across the Rhine.

Under the circumstances it was a strenuous exercise to keep reading between the lines of official pronouncements. Goethe was finding it difficult in any case to produce new work which the critics did not compare unfavourably with his earlier successes. He found it next to impossible to comment publicly on the Revolution. The most reasoned finished works which give his reactions only do so indirectly. He summarized his feelings as to the necessity to cleanse the Augean stables of the *ancien régime* in a minor play on the subject of the notorious pre-revolutionary scandal of the Queen's necklace and, further, made opportune use of the talents of an excellent comic actor temporarily appearing as a guest star with the Weimar troupe to stage a knockabout comedy on the subject of 'popular' government. His general mood of cynicism was doubtless also behind the interest with which he took up the medieval fable of Reynard the Fox, turning this into a not unskilful mock heroic poem in hexameters.

The striking feature about this poem was undoubtedly Goethe's turning to the hexameter. One might have imagined all kinds of directions in which the talents of the author of *Götz* might develop; but to find them moving back, as it might seem, towards a Classical form, struck many contemporaries as the most surprising development of all. But, to adapt a Brechtian image, a mountain-climber may have to backtrack if he finds himself at a great height following a blind path, and he may seem to be descending where he is merely looking for another way forward. This was the case now, not only with Goethe, but also with Schiller, who was to become his aesthetic adviser for the next decade. In both cases the departure from Classical practice had not been as final as readers of their first, revolutionary works imagined; the break with Classical style had simply been an expression of iconoclastic youth (expressed all the more stridently in Schiller's case because the young Swabian was ten years younger than Goethe and consequently absorbed the bookish 'subversion' of the Sturm und Drang generation whilst still a schoolboy).[29] There are signs all through that there was never any intention to throw Classicism overboard for good and all. But there was one very good reason why Goethe should turn to Classicism precisely in this post-revolutionary decade: Classicism suddenly seemed eminently desirable as a mark of stability in a world where all the obvious external signposts had started to reel, where the very ground on which men stood was quaking. Goethe had already begun to appreciate new virtues in Classicism during his Italian tour, where he ignored 'picturesque' ancient Italy and praised almost solely neo-classical and Classical Italy, notably Palladio in architecture and Raphael and Michelangelo in the graphic and plastic arts. This had not been without its impact on his literary production. Though his quickened creative impulse helped him finish off the northern *Egmont* and inspired him to compose new scenes for *Faust,* almost his main activity for the last year of his sabbatical was the work on *Iphigenie* and *Tasso,* and, in the case of the former drama notably, what this work entailed was a re-founding of the original torso of a drama, turning the prose scenes into rhymed ones – and these verse scenes were Classical from the outset.

There is little evidence that the small amount of poetry actually written in Italy made any special effort to be Classical. But the moment Goethe returned to Weimar, the spirit of Italy seemed to gain complete control of him. The verse in which he celebrated his new-found love for Christiane and his liaison with her are called *Römische Elegien*, and they show an intimate acquaintance with Latin poets of the stamp of Catullus, Propertius and Tibullus. The short visit to Italy in 1790 to take the place of Herder in accompanying the Dowager Duchess back home from her Italian journey was a great disillusionment for the poet: he had to rendezvous with the Dowager Duchess in Venice in midsummer, and the unhappy experience (which also took him away

[29] Another great influence on my generation was the work of Prof. L. A. Willoughby. This is demonstrated in a great mass of writing, but, in this connection, see his elegant and exhaustive edn of Schiller's *Die Räuber* (Oxford 1922).

from the young son who had just been born to Christiane) gave him black thoughts about the real modern Italy which he put down – again in Classical metres – in the *Venetianische Epigramme*. Classical metres now became, in fact, the repository for his *Zeitkritik*: what could not be said aloud in plain German prose was hinted at gnomically within the knotted framework of pseudo-classical satire. This was shown to the world in the turn (with Schiller) to the savage cultural criticism of the *Xenien* in 1796; hence the poet's beginning an epic poem on Achilles in 1797. The untimely death of the Weimar actress Christiane Neumann gave rise to the classically-worded elegy 'Euphrosyne' and, finally, Goethe's ultimate judgement on the French Revolution was given Classical form (poetic in both cases) in the verse novella *Hermann und Dorothea* (1796) and the tragedy *Die natürliche Tochter* (1803, started in 1797).[30]

Though Goethe is called the first great *modern* writer in nineteenth-century Germany, he grew into this role only slowly and to some extent against his inclination. The same can be said of Schiller's devolution from violent social rebel to courtier and author of a series of great tragedies built on faithful Boileauesque principles. This conscious backtracking of the two great contemporaries was nowhere more striking than in the early years of their collaboration in running the Weimar Theatre, when both of them translated and adapted for the German stage seventeenth-century French classical dramas; and Goethe even rewrote two poor tragedies by Voltaire.[31] Schiller's move towards Classicism had come during his year's sabbatical as guest of Christian Körner and his circle in Dresden: Körner, though a 'free spirit' in politics and philosophy, was in aesthetics very much a devotee of Saxon rococo and his enthusiasms communicated themselves to Schiller in this field as they did in the study of Kant's philosophical works.

[30] My own debt to Prof. R. H. Samuel, who was for three years my head of department at the University of Melbourne, is great. It is a pleasure to quote from the festal collection of his writings published in Melbourne in 1969. See, for this reference, the article on *Hermann und Dorothea*.

[31] See e. g. H. Knudsen, *Goethes Welt des Theaters* (Berlin 1949), and W. Fleming, *Goethes Gestaltung des klassischen Theaters* (Cologne 1949).

Schiller left Dresden re-converted, one might say. During his early years in the Duchy of Weimar, when, on Goethe's recommendation, he was appointed to a supernumerary Chair of History at Jena, this development continued inside him; it is not surprising therefore to find that the letter from Schiller to Goethe which ultimately brought the two men together as collaborators was an invitation from the younger man to join him in helping launch a new 'little magazine', to be called, significantly, *Die Horen*. Schiller's Classicism, like all his overblown enthusiasms, can become comically antiquarian at times, as when, in the ballad *Die Kraniche des Ibykus*, written in 1797 during the famous contest between the two friends over ballad-writing, he introduced allusions which even his contemporaries needed concordances to understand. Goethe rarely goes as far as this; the fact that each 'chapter' of *Hermann und Dorothea* is named after one of the Muses and partakes of the nature of the Muse mentioned was not a recherché allusion for his contemporaries, who were all educated in at least simple Classical poetic lore of this kind.

What was important for Goethe was that his return to Classicism was a return to artistic procedures which in his eyes gave him the ability to penetrate deeper into the explanation of Life. There is, after all, everything in Classical art which is necessary to interpret human nature, as we know it. What was wrong with the rococo age was that the writers approached their subject – Life – too superficially, using Classical forms as decorative ornamentation only. What Goethe attempted to do now was use Classical form to symbolize the importance of continuity and tradition whilst giving his own interpretations of the poet's material, Life. In this way he succeeded in giving an impressive panorama of the solidity of life in a small German market-town in *Hermann und Dorothea*, just as in the 1809 *Wahlverwandtschaften* he was to write one of the first modern psychological novels (about adultery, what is more) – but within a rigidly 'Classical' framework.

Die natürliche Tochter was a much more ambitious attempt to deal with the problems raised by the French Revolution, though it is difficult to judge the drama with finality because it is only part of what was intended to be either a two- or three-play sequence. But here, almost alone amongst the poet's works from these years, he faced the problems of living squarely and openly in revolution. In *Hermann* (as in the unfinished novella-sequence *Unterhaltungen deutscher Ausgewanderten*, 1797) the Revolution provides a background of general lawlessness and disorganization against which the solidity of the daily round in the smug burgher market-town stands out favourably. In the novella-sequence the tellers of the tales were to be a trek of German refugees from the Rhineland areas affected by invasion (replacing Boccaccio's plague-refugees from Florence). But in the tragedy the audience is brought right into the heart of the Revolution; the story tells of the illegitimate daughter of a duke whose assumption of her rightful role is prevented, on the one hand, by the machinations of her ambitious legitimate brother and, on the other hand, by the breakdown of society in the kingdom, where a revolution finally erupts. Here Goethe ultimately succeeded in finding an appealing objective correlative for his attitude to the great upheaval of his time: he was well aware of the precarious situation of the illegitimate child, fighting tenaciously to have his son August legitimized in 1802, four years before he brought himself to marry Christiane. The problems of class which his own liaison entailed were made a microcosm of society on the eve of the Revolution, and Goethe put them into words in his tragedy.[32]

The plot now takes a course away from autobiography. The scheming of the politicos sends the ill-fated heroine to a port from which she is to be shipped to malarial isles whence there can be no return (the incidents were actually based on a well-known autobiographical tale of the times which circulated under the name of a Princess de Bourbon-Conti). After the heroine has appealed in vain to various strata of the population for help, she finally finds refuge – unwillingly and despairingly – in marriage

[32] *Die natürliche Tochter* has suffered from a reputation for being convoluted and dull. A survey of the relevant literature will be found in an article of mine on the drama in *Proc. Eng. Goethe Soc.* (1970–1). Some shrewd remarks on Goethe's feelings about class are to be found in the popular but not always scholarly Goethe biography by R. Friedenthal (Weidenfeld 1965).

with an upstanding representative of the commercial middle classes. The drama ends here, on a note of resignation which is eloquent of Goethe's intellectual development in these years and also mirrors his feeling of having lost all sense of glamour in love. But it would seem that the sequel was to show an even more interesting dialectical turn to the plot: the illegitimate princess was to find, as she grows to respect and love her enforced husband, that he is more and more deeply involved in plotting on behalf of the bourgeois revolution. Despite her love for him, however, she was to return to the capital to testify on behalf of her own class (despite its ill treatment of her) and to perish beside the King (probably) on the scaffold.

Here Goethe said what he had to say about the Revolution. He realized that the *ancien régime* was rotten and deserved to be made to give way to the rule of the decent bourgeoisie. But he had been taught by experience that history is only made by individuals: the vagaries of the actual history of his own day were, he saw, a result of the fates of myriads of individuals (this was an attitude which Büchner was to demonstrate much more clearly – though perhaps not even yet clearly enough for average audiences – using as his model a completely de-glamorized Danton). Above all, Goethe had finally matured in thought to the point of accepting the fact that history invariably breaks its puppets; the individual can ultimately hope at best only to know that he had good intentions and to resign himself to the nonsense fate has made of his own life. This philosophy was often discussed with Schiller, for the latter's mind was moving on a much more intellectual plane in the same direction.

The moralistic Swabian even went so far as to write his *Briefe über die ästhetische Erziehung des Menschen* in the hope of being able to *persuade* men with words to make themselves worthier than the French had proved themselves to be of undertaking revolution in their countries.[33] But in addition he also poured his thoughts into drama. A tragedy, *Don Carlos*, which had started, in his own words, as a 'bourgeois tragedy in a royal

[33] See especially E. M. Wilkinson's introduction and notes to her English translation *On the Aesthetic Education of Man* (Oxford 1967). This was done in collaboration with L. A. Willoughby.

milieu' – showing the hopeless love of the Infante Don Carlos for his prospective bride Elisabeth of Valois after she had become the wife of his father Philip II of Spain, was refashioned to take up what had earlier been a merely subsidiary motif, showing Don Carlos' involvement against his father in the contemporary Revolt of the Netherlands. This political plot dominates the second half of the tragedy and shows Schiller too demonstrating how the purest of reformers becomes bogged down by events and frustrated by human evil. This theme was to be stated much more clearly in Schiller's great Wallenstein trilogy which he was writing at the time when the *rapprochement* with Goethe finally took place. The figure of Wallenstein emerged from the historical research on which Schiller had engaged at the university of Jena: like Goethe he had started by studying the last great popular revolution before the eighteenth century, the Dutch freedom campaign. Goethe had made this the background for his *Egmont*: Schiller for his part made it the subject of a brilliant historical monograph. He went on to look at contemporary Germany, studying the seeds of Germany's eighteenth-century discontents in the tragic catastrophe of the Thirty Years War.

Unlike Goethe, who concentrated on a subsidiary figure (destined, however, to play a leading role at the end), Schiller turned his attention to the leading actor himself. His play is solely about Wallenstein, the demonic general of the Catholic forces. Schiller's dramatic genius, however, ultimately drove him to realize that this 'bourgeois tragedy in a political milieu' was inadequate to represent the full sweep of the popular life of the early seventeenth century: as a result he added the brilliant panorama of a military camp which became *Wallensteins Lager*, an independent prologue to the two dramas making up the actual play. Had Goethe finally done as much for *Die natürliche Tochter*, he could indeed have created a masterly allegory for the French Revolution.

How far Goethe and Schiller had gone in the direction of the Classical revival can be studied in the actual form of this play. That Goethe was aware of what he was doing is clear from the fact that he deliberately bound *Die natürliche Tochter* with *Iphigenie* and *Tasso* in the 1808 edition of his works. The form, however, is even severer and plainer than that of the two earlier works. It is possible to see in what he produced here the influence of his simultaneous preoccupation with the practical work of the Weimar Theatre. Throughout the time of his collaboration with Schiller their aim was to develop a superior form of theatre, anything but realistic in approach; many contemporaries, in fact, took exception to the strictness with which naturalistic acting was kept off the Weimar stage and the extent to which the Weimar troupe was trained in stylized gesture and declamation. Simultaneously with *Die natürliche Tochter*, Schiller produced a tragedy which is almost ludicrous in its strict adherence to a now outworn classical convention, *Die Braut von Messina.* What Schiller tried to do with the Greek Chorus in this tragedy, Goethe tried in *Die natürliche Tochter* to do with an approach in which non-naturalism was heightened. As a result he brings the drama's effect into the vicinity of Brechtian 'alienation', the style in which the audience is incited to react to the events with their minds but not through their sympathy with flesh-and-blood characters.

It was necessary to enter into this discussion of a purely literary technique in order to underline the importance which the Revolutionary period, even in this indirect way, had for Goethe's general state of mind. From the turn of the century it should be added that Goethe followed the rise of Napoleon with growing admiration. Though today some people consider that Napoleon stemmed the course of the Revolution, to contemporaries the Emperor was continuing the work of Mirabeau, Robespierre and Danton; this was what Goethe honoured him for. The sickening uncertainties of the Reign of Terror were now replaced by a firm revolutionary will, even if it was united with a display of external pomp and, ultimately, with political manœuvring and military campaigns which trampled on the national aspirations of sympathetic Europe. The link between the Revolution and the burgeoning nationalism of Europe is reflected in Schiller's tragedies, where we see national movements in action in France, in Switzerland and in Russia, for instance : Goethe saw the national ferment at work and appreciated it (for example, in the work of Manzoni, Mickiewicz and Scott), but it did not sour him in his appreciation of Napoleon. His hero-worship reached its culmination in 1806 when he had a series of interviews with the conqueror at the great Imperial court at Erfurt. Unlike the sceptical Wieland (who did not bother to change out of his house-slippers to meet the great man), Goethe had learnt to use court ceremonial as a barrier against untoward intrusions into his personal privacy – which gave him a reputation for stiffness and even snobbery. He deeply appreciated the fact that at Erfurt Napoleon gave him almost more time than he gave to any German sovereign. His close contact with the Emperor certainly confirmed his belief (expressed later to Eckermann) that the writer must *be* someone in order to be able to create great literature, and that he develops as a person when allowed to come close to great men and, as he put it, look over their shoulders and see the cards in their hands.

Goethe had one other entrée into 'great thoughts'. When poetic inspiration ran dry and the outside world was unappetizing, he took refuge in the study of natural science. Introduced at an early age to alchemy, at university to medicine and, in his capacity as a civil servant, to mineralogy, he grew more and more interested in natural objects as he grew older. He contributed, as did many of his contemporaries, to different branches which today require specialists for their understanding (like his near-contemporary Albrecht von Haller, the great physiologist, who reviewed for his journal some 9000 learned works, covering all the arts and sciences, over the course of his life). Whilst it can no longer be held that Goethe was a great original scientist, he certainly was in the van of many of the scientific movements of his day, as in his famous discovery – contemporary with similar discoveries made by other scientists of the day who were unknown to him – of the intermaxillary bone, the link between human and animal evolution. In one field Goethe made great and original contributions to new thought without succeeding in gaining the respect of the experts: this was the field of optics where he published his *Farbenlehre* (the first part in 1791). It was perhaps to be expected that a creative artist – and a painter, to boot – should take exception to Newton's mechanistic wave theory of colour.

Goethe's theory of colour is much more creative and delves

deeply into the dialectic of light and shade as the source of our subjective feelings of colouring. Though modern developments in the higher reaches of atomic theory have, without shaking it, cast some discredit on the Newtonian theory, we may well say that Goethe's researches were less valuable to science than to his own development; in particular, they gave him distraction during the revolutionary wars. He would otherwise have been hard pressed to maintain mental equilibrium; but he took his scientific work with him into the field and was occupied during the Valmy campaign much more with optics and anatomy than with strategy.

From the literary standpoint the most important aspect of his scientific work was his constant preoccupation with the real workings of Nature – expressed beautifully, for example, in the long poem 'Metamorphose der Pflanzen' (1790), written to explain to the illiterate Christiane his pre-evolutionary botanical theory as to the way in which the entire form and nature of plants arise from the basic shape of the leaf. This sort of activity, marrying acute observation and verbal inspiration, runs through a very great deal of his poetic output at this time, giving the lyrics of his middle and later period their delightful mixture of beauty and faithfulness to nature.

Chapter 9

Classical Doubts and Achievements

We have now actually accompanied Goethe up into his sixties. He was universally acclaimed as Germany's greatest creative writer and was beginning to become a centre for pilgrimage, as always happens to great writers who have the good fortune to live long lives. On what did this reputation rest? It must not be thought that a literary reputation such as Goethe's was gained without opposition. At the time when the poet first made his reputation, that is, in the period normally called the Sturm und Drang, the appearance of *Werther* and *Götz* called forth hostility and satirical criticism from dyed-in-the-wool representatives of the rationalistic Enlightenment, such as Lessing's old friend and collaborator, Nicolai, the publisher in Berlin. Yet Goethe had the young and the female readers solidly on his side. But youth is a stuff which does not, it is known, endure, and, as Goethe matured and became more and more judicious in his comments on the passing scene, the general public tended to give its acclaim to other – younger – voices.

Goethe's fame was bolstered at first by the appearance, ten years after his own first-fruits, of Schiller's Sturm und Drang works. But Schiller too set out on the same long climb from the lush plains of youthful revolt up to the more rarified heights of regretful contemplation. Then, in the vivid aftermath of the French Revolution, a new and aggressive generation took the stage. Ironically enough these young men, led by a group which had come together at the Weimar state university at Jena –

the brothers Schlegel and Friedrich von Hardenberg (who wrote under the pseudonym Novalis), to be joined soon by the Berliner Ludwig Tieck – considered themselves to be the defenders of Goethe's youthful views against his – ossified – later work. Moreover, the shrewd Friedrich Schlegel realized that the younger men needed to show a spirit of attack on and criticism of the old order so as to establish themselves as innovators. This aggressiveness somewhat tarnished Goethe's image, though the actual point of the attacks was ostensibly directed against the more vulgarly popular Wieland (who continued his vast outflow of novels and verse right up to his death in 1813) rather than against Goethe and Schiller.[34] More direct hostility to Goethe came only at this stage from the Berlin rationalist critics, and notably from the popular playwright August von Kotzebue, who needed to denigrate Goethe in order to establish his own lightweight personality.

But perhaps the greatest damage to Goethe's reputation was that done by the poet himself in respect of what he published during the 1780s and 1790s. In fact, it would be more to the point to say that he published almost no major work during this period. He contributed verse to very many 'little magazines' and reviews and essays to scientific journals. But the only major works made accessible to the public – and this not until a collected edition of his works came out in the 1790s – were *Iphigenie* and *Tasso*.

Goethe's return to the Classical forms can be seen today as a logical evolution of his genius. To the younger generation of his contemporaries it came as an unpleasant shock. The reaction against Classicism which seemed to have been made by the dramas and novels of the Sturm und Drang period had continued to gain ground amongst the young. It was pursued by the Schlegel group (increasingly called 'Romantics' in opposition to the 'Classics'). Novalis took up the loose form of *Werther* in his enormous and rambling novel *Heinrich von Ofterdingen*, blending into it elements of fairy fantasy which had been popularized

[34] There is a thorough investigation of the motives behind the attacks made by the Romantics in F. Sengle, *Wieland* (Stuttgart 1949).

by Wieland in particular; Wieland found that there was a market for fantasy, amongst female readers especially, and so he increasingly – either satirically or as delicate caprices – modernized pastoral elements from rococo popular literature. It was perhaps a reaction to the horrors of the Revolution and the subsequent warfare which thus brought into popularity this fairy-tale genre. One of the most extraordinary developments in the vein was to be seen in the work of Tieck, for this young writer was first commissioned by Nicolai to produce satires on the work of the Sturm und Drang : but he developed his particular vein of fantasy (first intended as satire) into a genre in its own right. Novalis, Brentano and, amongst slightly later writers, notably E. T. A. Hoffmann, were to follow Tieck successfully into the realms of Fairyland. Tieck also attempted, in his *Gestiefelter Kater* (Puss-in-Boots) to bring the fairy world on to the stage.

It was only a step from this vein of fantasy to what contemporary literary critics were to call the Exotic. The eighteenth century had also been interested in contributions from outside Europe – as the blending of Chinese motives into the rococo shows. Wieland constantly made excursions into exotic mythologies (Persian, Mexican, Chinese) to give piquancy to his invention. For the Romantics there was the further development that in their hostility to the Greek and Roman Classical they lighted on the work of the great Spanish dramatists of the seventeenth century. The Spaniards had another charm in their eyes, moreover : they were artefacts which breathed intense religious fervour – and a fervour of a specifically Roman Catholic kind. Though Novalis notably came from a devoutly Protestant family, there is an intensity about his ideas which in more unstable temperaments turned easily into Roman Catholic mysticism (many of the Romantic writers actually became converts, whilst Brentano, born into a very rationalistic Roman Catholic household, returned so wholeheartedly to mystical beliefs that he spent the final years of his life acting as amanuensis to an inspired nun).[35]

[35] There are no really illuminating general treatments of the German Romantic writers. Willoughby's *Romantic Movement in Germany* (Oxford 1930) is still as good as anything published since.

If one compares the weird lucubrations of the young men of the 1790s with the increasingly sober approach and palette of the ageing Goethe, it can be seen that the master's reputation was becoming the kind of public acceptance which, unless bolstered by continuous new work, is suddenly 'unmasked' one day by some critic looking for the emperor's new clothes and failing to find them. In the end Goethe did produce more works of genius to show the validity of his reputation; but the works were spread out widely, and they were attacked, as they appeared, for varying reasons by opponents from the most varying literary schools.

Goethe's two most strictly Classical dramas were given their final shape during the poet's stay in Italy. Both had been started during the early years in Weimar, if not earlier. A prose version of *Iphigenie* was performed in Weimar in 1779 and there is evidence that *Tasso* may rest on the foundations of a play which was begun even before *Werther*, but which was certainly written (or perhaps rewritten) between March 1780 and November 1781. These two fragments, plus the more obviously Sturm und Drang *Egmont*, we know to have been manuscripts in Goethe's Italian baggage. *Egmont* and scenes of the *Urfaust* were amongst his special preoccupations during his Italian wanderings, but it was the two former plays, rewritten in the last half of his journey and revised on his return to Weimar, which show what might be considered more obvious signs of 'Classical' influence. In respect of Goethe's reputation it may, moreover, be noted that *Faust* was still unknown to the general public (and to all but a very restricted Weimar court circle) until *Faust. Ein Fragment* was published in 1790 in the series of the poet's collected works, whilst *Egmont*, softened though the sentiments were by comparison with the productions of the 1770s, still has an air of belonging to the *Geniezeit* despite the fact that it was not published until it appeared as one volume of the collected works in 1788.

It could as such still attract the young men who identified themselves, generation after generation, with Werther and his author. To these the new Classical plays seemed almost a slap in the face. Yet it would seem that the origins of *Tasso* lie close to those of the great novel: Goethe himself called the drama '*gesteigerter Werther*'. According to H. M. Wolff[36] *Tasso* too began as the story of a *Genie* struggling against a man of 'merely normal' talents, for power and the love of one woman. This interpretation certainly brings some kind of order into many of the strange logical breaks in the final version of the play and also gives a meaning to the odd double ending (where one speech is a valorous vindication of being a poet: '*Gab mir ein Gott zu sagen, wie ich leide*'; the last half a pessimistic shipwrecked cry of despair).

According to this reading, three periods of work on the play can be observed. The first is the Wertheresque story which could be the drama on a subject of this kind mentioned in a letter from the poet to Kestner in 1773; this manuscript travelled to Weimar with Goethe and was then completely rethought in the light of Goethe's turn to platonic love under the influence of Frau von Stein, as well as being re-drafted as a result of his concrete experience of life at an enlightened court. We know nothing of these two versions, although there is evidence that only the first two acts were entirely re-cast in 1780–1: the fact that Goethe stopped at this point and could not continue was due to the poet's sluggishness in working out the plot – something which held up the decisive plotting of *Faust* for so many decades. The difficulty was obviously that the Tasso whom Goethe invented in his Sturm und Drang youth and, above all Antonio, his counterpart, the saturnine figure of the embodied philistine (for whom the unfortunate Kestner had to stand as model in *Werther*), no longer corresponded to Goethe's experience of how poets and their rivals behaved at court.

Only in Italy was Goethe enabled to harmonize these elements and to weave around his earlier outline a more satisfactory tapestry. Work was carried on from 1787 until 1789 and the final version was published in the collected works in December of this last year. It makes a satisfactory five-act Classical play even if there are sufficient loose ends to have worried the critics for years, and an ending which calls forth all Dr Gray's philo-

[36] Wolff, op. cit. (*Goethes Weg . . .*) and Braemer, op. cit. (*Goethes Prometheus . . .*).

sophical powers and vituperative analysis.[37] The Italian air enabled Goethe to give great charm and suavity to the plotting, whilst the revival of his emotional powers of expression as a result of breaking with Frau von Stein enabled him once more to summon up the feelings of a poet harassed beyond bearing by the philistinism of an unfeeling world. The fact that this is not motivated fully by what actually happens in the play must in the long run be considered less important than the 'Classical' serenity which, despite the tragic subject, permeates the whole. In this final version the story is almost unbelievably simple. The harassed poet Torquato Tasso has found shelter at the court of the enlightened Prince Alfonso of Ferrara. Antonio, the Prince's chief minister, returns from a successful diplomatic mission and at once falls foul of the unworldly poet. The quarrel reaches a climax when the poet breaks court convention by drawing his sword on the diplomat, and falls into disgrace. This might not seem too tragic, but there is a vital parallel subject: Tasso is faced at the court by two female admirers, the Prince's sister and her friend or lady-in-waiting, both called Leonora. The friend is a lively but shallow society lady; the Princess a paragon of Platonic virtue. Frenzied by his other worries and teased by the friend, Tasso imagines himself more and more into a state of intense love for the Princess and in the last act once more shatters court protocol by embracing her. His disgrace is irreversible and complete; what is more, he is made to realize that what has happened to him – in both cases – has been due to lack of self-control. He undergoes the humiliation of having to acknowledge this in public, and the play ends on a tragic note which is resolved only by the poet's realization that, however deep he may have fallen, it is he (and not the others) who has the divine power of poetry. Goethe obviously did not succeed in resolving all the problems which had gone into the weaving of this plot. But he did succeed in giving the language and the plotting that wonderfully serene charm which is the magic external mark of

[37] R. D. Gray, *Goethe: A Critical Introduction* (Cambridge 1967) contains a series of attacks on almost all Goethe's works, being written from the empyrean standpoint of the 'Cambridge' criticism associated with the followers of F. R. Leavis.

modern 'Classicism'. Those who are susceptible to the language felt this and applauded the finished product. To the general public it was (and has remained) a strange and unsubstantial subject.[38]

The same is true, in many ways, of *Iphigenie auf Tauris*, though here the poet was much more successful in producing a harmonious whole. Goethe was helped by having chosen a traditional subject which he only needed to reinterpret to make psychologically plausible according to contemporary lights. The prose version of 1779 clearly contained much of the storminess of the Sturm und Drang: Iphigenia, daughter of King Agamemnon, was to be sacrificed to the gods in order to induce favourable winds for the Greek fleet. But the goddess Diana spirited her away to Tauris (in the Crimea) where she lived as High Priestess in the goddess's temple. Her brother Orestes, whom she had left as an infant, had in the meantime carried out his role in the ghastly sequence of events which was wished on Agamemnon's family. He had avenged his father's murder on Clytemnestra, his abandoned mother, but the Furies had driven him away in madness from the scene of his crime. He and his bosom friend are now washed up on the shores of Tauris, just at the moment when the Scythian king Thoas has grown weary of Iphigenia's long years of refusing his offers of marriage: he orders her to revert to the original barbarian custom, which she had had abolished, of sacrificing on the altar all shipwrecked strangers. In the Greek original brother and sister escape from their captivity, bearing away the sacred statue of Diana. Goethe was not interested in this story as he found it but concentrated on the role played by the sister: for her magic presence at once cures her brother of his madness. The final denouement he brought about with a cavalier disregard for psychological *vraisemblance* which generations of critics have found it easy enough to condemn – Iphigenia turns her magic serenity on the barbarian Thoas and pleads with him to allow her to leave Tauris with the Greeks. Goethe makes him agree with the laconic words *'Lebt wohl!'* – which really give no clue as to his real reactions, although we may accept that it is Iphigenia's pure humanity which has persuaded him.

[38] See R. Peacock, *Goethe's Major Plays* (Manchester 1959).

Once again, however, the important fact about this play is its atmosphere. There is hardly any other of his works in which the magic of Goethe's style is more generously spread out before the audience. For this reason what today appears as a basically most 'Romantic' treatment of the Greek legend could appear to contemporaries as a serenely 'Classical' creation. Goethe covered the surface of his tragedy with a glittering filigree of poetry, just as Shakespeare made the cheap melodrama of Macbeth palatable through the power of his words. The form is strictly Classical: there are five acts which are divided up according to the most Racinian of dramatic arithmetic. The first act introduces the story of Iphigenia; the second brings Orestes and Pylades on to the stage. The third act works out the confrontation of brother and sister and, as the pivot-act, demonstrates the healing of the frenzied Orestes in a most powerful monologue of great length. In the fourth act the problem of safe departure casts shadows on the plot and Iphigenia seems to be convinced by Pylades' arguments that she must tell a lie to Thoas in order to gain them all a stealthy exit. Having passed through a hell of decision-making, in the fifth act Iphigenia finally opts for absolute truth and thus gains freedom for the Greeks.

In many ways this dramatic structure is the most absolute of all the rationalist dramas of the Enlightenment – as logical in its symmetry as Racine's *Andromaque*. But the sheer beauty of the language masks the deliberate nature of the structure: thus Goethe makes masterly use of the small area of lyricism allowed by Corneille and Racine through the ability to change metre and introduce what are essentially lyrical arias into the normal progress of the plot. His rhythmical insertions culminate in the magnificently sombre *Parzenlied* (song of the Parcae, or Furies) in which Iphigenia pours out her tormented conscience at the end of act five. The device was to stay in the poet's mind and to recur on an even grander scale in the final version of *Faust*, where Gretchen's progress is underlined by no fewer than four such lyrical interludes.

It is surprising that so Romantic an outpouring of emotions – a drama, moreover, staged in a Scythia which is so patently a rococo theatrical set – should have seemed disappointing to contemporaries. One must remember, however, that in 1789 news of the French Revolution was already beginning to seep through into Germany, so that such a perfectly finished surface seemed unfeeling in its perfection. The spectators were also the very people who were beginning to dabble their toes in the exotic waters of Romantic fairy-tale: on the stage itself popular taste was being fed with two streams gushing from the very success of the *Geniezeit* – domestic tragedies which owed everything to *Werther* in spirit (and to the spiritual progenitor of the Sturm und Drang, Lessing, in form); and so-called '*Ritterstücke*', mock-medieval chivalric dramas, which owed everything to *Götz*.

This misunderstanding was not even cleared up by the publication of the fragmentary version of *Faust* in 1790, partly because the public was not expecting such a production at this point in Goethe's collected works, and partly because the fragment as such was not obviously a tragedy for the stage. A similar misunderstanding was to bedevil (and still bedevils) Goethe's other major production of this period, the verse novella *Hermann und Dorothea*, published in 1794. In many ways this is the most programmatically Classical product of Goethe's maturity: there would seem to be almost a spirit of perversity in his having cast what is manifestly the first contribution to that great German form, the nineteenth-century Novelle, into Homeric hexameters. Nor is Goethe entirely without responsibility if he was mildly misunderstood, since he not only used Greek metre for his tale; he also made lavish use of Homeric devices, such as the frequently repeated 'stock' epithet to describe the individual characters. The fact that this was an ironic device, possibly inspired in the craftsman Goethe by his work on updating the medieval beast-epic *Reinecke Fuchs* the previous year, has never been accepted by the public as an excuse: Goethe here fell a victim to one of the great laws of public life, namely that irony is not a device which the mass audience either likes or wishes to understand.

It has long been accepted that the history of the nineteenth-century Novelle begins with Goethe, though E. K. Bennett,[39] for example, chose as his avatar the fairy-tale-like story to which

[39] E. K. Bennett, *The History of the German Novelle* (Cambridge 1961).

Goethe simply gave the name 'Novelle' and which he produced in 1824. More recent critics have preferred to refer to various episodes of *Wilhelm Meisters Wanderjahre* or to parts of the earlier *Unterhaltungen deutscher Ausgewanderten.* None of these has the power allied with simplicity of the story of *Hermann und Dorothea.* As R. H. Samuel has noted,[40] in this episode Goethe was dealing not with symbolical figures (as in so many of the *Meister* tales or in the 'Novelle' itself), or with equally abstracted episodes concerning aristocratic participants with whom he could not entirely identify himself. In this work Goethe tells an unvarnished tale about people of exactly his own stamp, solid German middle class. This, of course, makes the Classical framework all the more incongruous.

Despite the simplicity of the tale and the genuineness of its psychological structure, the actual plotting is intricate. Goethe divided the poem into nine cantos (each superscribed with the name of one of the Muses and partaking of the character of the particular Muse), and the plot-structure falls symmetrically into four stages on either side of the great central canto, the fourth canto paralleling the first, and so on. Over this structure the poet spread his story: Hermann, the still dependent son of a trusty small-town innkeeper and town councillor, is sent to give charity to refugees encamped just outside the town. In the original source these were Protestant refugees from a tyrannical Catholic archbishop of Salzburg. Just as Goethe transplanted the town where the story takes place from Saxony to the countryside of his beloved Main, so now he transmuted the original Austrian refugees into much more symbolical German refugees fleeing the revolutionary troubles on the left bank of the Rhine in the area of Mainz (the city where a French-style commune was introduced). These matters only lend greater depth and resonance to the happenings which are important for the poem: Hermann falls in love with a sturdy refugee who is mothering the trek (as Lotte was acting as mother to her family when Werther first met her). In the first half of the story he struggles with his blustering father to gain permission to launch (very abruptly) into the serious business of matrimony – and to marry a complete stranger of dubious ante-

[40] Samuel on *Hermann und Dorothea,* as before (n.30).

cedents. Having overcome parental objections with the help of his splendid mother (a resounding tribute to Goethe's own solid mother, Frau Aja) and some Dickensian family friends, Hermann passes through the agony of having to ask Dorothea to marry him. The chapter of misunderstandings entailed by the boy's shyness fills the last four cantos.

It should be noted that the verse-novel as a genre is nothing like as exotic an art form as one might imagine. This was particularly so at this period as a result of the widespread popularity of the rococo pastoral tale (and its much-loved branch, the idyll). One may note particularly Crabbe's *Peter Grimes,* Pushkin's *Eugene Onegin*, Wieland's *Oberon* and Byron's *Don Juan.* Even today the fashion is not entirely dead : the Expressionists revived it round the turn of the century (Hauptmann, Döblin, Alexander Blok), Tvardovski had a great war-time success with it in the Soviet Union, and, most recently, Philip Toynbee has once more returned to it.

The fact remains that *Hermann und Dorothea* did not add to Goethe's reputation to the extent of blotting out his fame as author of *Werther*. Nothing was to do that. Even the spreading reputation of *Faust* did not at first make Goethe once more an integral part of Europe's popular culture. (Not, that is, until later in the nineteenth century when *Faust* eclipsed the rest of Goethe's works to an extent which still obscures his name as the author of other masterpieces.) But the praise which the works mentioned in this chapter gained for him did contribute to keeping up this reputation, so that in 1809 he could enter his seventh decade as the continuing master of German literature.

Chapter 10

Poet in a Post-Revolutionary Landscape

When George Henry Lewes, Goethe's greatest English biographer, visited Weimar in the 1850s, within a short time, after all, of the poet's lifetime, he and his 'wife' (the novelist George Eliot) found the town tiny and not un-squalid.[41] If this was the case *after* the general rise in the German standard of living which followed the upheavals of 1830, it is difficult to envisage the low level of amenities at which, by English criteria, Goethe must have lived, despite his privileged position, especially in the period around 1800, when he was still settling himself into his (by Weimar standards) 'grand' town-house on the Frauenplan (a fairly wide curved cobbled street). Even today the house – now maintained by the German Democratic Republic as a splendidly, if tendentiously, equipped museum of the Goethezeit – tells its own story.

Outside, its two storeys are built of unpretentious yellow limestone and its considerable length follows the curve of the street. At one end is a larger opening which gave carriages entrance to a small court at the rear. The rest of the back forms a remarkably small flower-garden. The main entrance is by no means sumptuous. It is reached by a short double flight of some dozen steps and consists of a single simply-panelled front door overhung by a small Classical pediment. The sole sign of unusual sumptuousness is the fact that the house is rather longer than the normal

[41] G. H. Lewes, *The Life and Works of Goethe*, has been available in Dent's 'Everyman' series since 1908.

burgher house. In fact the atmosphere of this part of Weimar is no different from that of many German provincial towns whose burgher houses were built in the late eighteenth and early nineteenth centuries: this is the German equivalent of the English Queen Anne 'new town'.

Within, the house shows, of course, much more the stamp of its great owner. The rooms are tiny: it is significant that even the scrupulously detailed diarist Eckermann seldom reports anything in the nature of a large gathering. The usual afternoon or evening party was restricted to two or three intimates of the house. They might be joined by one or two visiting pilgrims, either from more distant parts of Germany or, as so very often, from abroad: in the 1820s it is clear, from Eckermann's career in Weimar, that Goethe's fame made Weimar into a centre for young Englishmen desirous of spending some months in Germany to learn the language. Some of these were well connected – they included notably young Lockhart, Walter Scott's future son-in-law, as well as the future editor of *The Times*, Henry Crabb Robinson. The actual receptions which were held were only a little larger than this, but on these occasions the folding doors between the rooms would be opened out to provide more space for the guests. There were times, for instance during visits by the Polish pianist Maria Szymanowska (to whom *Aussöhnung*, the third of the 'Trilogie der Leidenschaft' poems is dedicated), or by the young Felix Mendelssohn (highly recommended to Goethe by his Berlin musician friend C. F. Zelter, who had been the boy's piano teacher), or by Weimar's resident musician Hummel, when it was the room with the tiny pianoforte which was the centre of interest. But in general the two rooms in which the poet spent most of his time, either alone or with his friends, were his study and his print-room.

The study (like the single bedroom which the poet used after the death of Christiane) may be said to justify those simple-minded German Lutherans who draw from Goethe's life a moral of quiet devotion to duty. It is unbelievably bare compared with the studies which may be seen in this country in comparatively modest stately homes, such as Walter Scott's at Abbotsford. Compared with Wordsworth's chintzy cottage at Grassmere, it is spartan: the floor, as in Goethe's bedroom, is uncarpeted. Apart from one high-backed wooden armchair there are only kitchen chairs; we know in fact that Goethe did not work at a desk in a sitting position. His writing surface was placed on top of a row of cupboards containing manuscripts and other files; the poet sat at it, when he stopped walking round, on the kind of high stool once used by clerks in counting-houses. But, of course, Goethe did not himself write most of his own works after 1800 – he dictated them, as he dictated most of his voluminous correspondence and even his diaries. He had a succession of secretaries who became an integral part of his household – the last and most long-lived of them, J. A. F. John, is one of the two companions referred to in the closing stanzas of the 'Marienbader Elegie'; the other was Krause, his valet for many years.[42]

Goethe occupied only the ground and first floors of the house. As his son August grew, he lived more and more on the second floor, which was the domain at first of Christiane and her family. Later, when August married, he and his vivacious young wife[43] took over the whole of the second floor, and after his death it was here that the young widow continued to live for many years, enlivening the sorrow-darkened life of her father-in-law; but she also suddenly flew out of Weimar, to go to Genoa and, ultimately, to marry one of her many English visitors and cavaliers, Shelley's former friend, the young Charles Stirling.

Goethe could not be said to have lived a life of riotous gaiety in these somewhat severe surroundings, rendered all the more severe by the cold pomp of the Classical-style furniture which fills them. Taking over from his father a fondness for Greek

[42] The outstanding edn of Eckermann's *Gespräche mit Goethe* is that by H. H. Houben, (Berlin 1949). I am preparing a new one which was to have been for Prof. Grumach, to fit into the complete series of Goethe 'conversations' which he was editing before his death. Houben also produced Riemer's Goethe reminiscences and the authentic text of Soret's diaries. His two-volume biography of Eckermann is highly recommended. The 'Everyman' translation is being re-edited with an introduction by Prof. Roy Pascal, to whom, as my tutor and friend, I should also like to pay tribute here, especially in view of his early retirement.

[43] On Ottilie von Goethe see notably H. Bluhm in *Proc. Eng. Goethe Soc.*, Vol. XXVIII (1960), pp. 25–39.

and Roman sculpture, he filled the rooms with statuary, including a massive cast of the vastly larger-than-life Ludovisi Juno head. It is impossible to feel anything but constricted in these surroundings, so much less warm than the Dutch-style homeliness of the Goethe family home on the Hirschgraben in Frankfurt.

One wonders whether it was not unease in these surroundings which led the poet to spend so much of his later life in travelling. Almost every year he passed the summer months out of Weimar, following after 1806 the growing tendency of the Central European aristocracy to patronize the watering-places of the Sudetenland, Teplitz, Karlsbad and Marienbad. Sometimes his journeyings took him further afield still and he inspected geological and other sites in many parts of Bohemia. He made trips to the West as well. Two of these retraced the route of his Sturm und Drang journey to Switzerland, and in his leisurely progress round the cantons he made new friends, including, for example, the wellborn lady writer Barbara Schulthess, from whose possessions the manuscript of *Wilhelm Meisters Theatralische Sendung* was recovered only some sixty years ago. Other journeys took him to nearer resorts – one to the Sauerland spa, Bad Pyrmont; semi-official visits took him for lengthy periods to Ilmenau and Jena, and visits were paid to the courts of the minor Saxon dukes, Dessau, Gotha, Eisenach and so on. During the wars, when Weimar was once more threatened with French invasion, the poet was even persuaded to move east and found himself ultimately in Leipzig and Dresden.[44]

Perhaps the most emotional of these journeyings were, however, those which he undertook in 1814 and 1815 to his birthplace, Frankfurt, and the Rhenish area beyond. It is not only that his life was splendidly rejuvenated here by his encounter with Marianne von Willemer; he had the comfort of being reminded constantly of his youth and his sparkling mother in Frankfurt, and, in the Rhineland, contact with some of the leading figures in the German national revival. Among these was the great statesman, Karl, Freiherr von Stein, who entertained him at his

[44] Complete documentation plus maps in A. Zastrau, *Goethe-Handbuch* (Stuttgart 1955 –). As far as I know, there have been no further volumes since the fourth.

castle near Nassau and took him in his coach to see the remains of Cologne Cathedral, about to be rebuilt as a result of the enthusiasm of the great Romantic antiquarian Sulpiz Boisserée, whose family, Huguenot by origin, had now become Roman Catholic. Indeed, Boisserée had gone out of his way to obtain the great Goethe's support for his building plans and his enthusiasm undoubtedly opened Goethe's eyes, probably for the first time (it is difficult not to accept Robson-Scott's arguments that Goethe's paeans to the cathedral at Strasbourg were really directed to the Classical beauties in its structure), to the world of Gothic art and architecture. Boisserée was one of the first great collectors of early German and Italian art and, when he visited the Boisserée home in Cologne (Köln), Goethe seems to have been perceptibly touched by the beauty of what he saw there.[45]

Undoubtedly the most productive of these journeyings, from the literary standpoint, were the two summer visits to Frankfurt which resulted ultimately in the production of the poetic collection called the *Westöstlicher Divan*.[46] The poet developed in his later life an interesting theory to interpret poetic genius, noting, amongst other things, that the genius needs above all what Goethe called the faculty of enjoying a 'repeated puberty'. What he meant by this was that an ageing genius, such as he had been – from the time of his Italian journey, if one measures by contemporary standards – still has the ability to fall in love again and again with the tremulous freshness of a young poet in his teens. For most of us the age of puberty is associated largely with the pains of adjustment to grown-up life; but puberty is also the time when we become conscious of the opposite sex for the first time and, if we are poets, set down on paper the hesitant feelings of lyrical pleasure and pain which this new experience causes. Sometimes, if we are a Keats or a Ronsard, this enables us to say lasting things about this world, which we have suddenly seen with new eyes, which posterity will share with us for ever. But men age, and feelings wither. Goethe's contention was that he, and other great poets who continue to write lyric poetry in

[45] Robson-Scott, op. cit. (n. 15).

[46] U. Wertheim, *Von Tasso bis Hafis* (Berlin 1965).

their maturer years, constantly revive this early magic whenever their affections are re-engaged.

This subject has often been a matter for joking. But we find in Goethe's letters nothing but a most serious approach to his new-found 'shepherdesses', even when, as in the case of Sylvie von Ziegesar and Minna Herzlieb, he found happiness for a succession of summers with them whilst *still* enjoying the domestic happiness of his marriage with Christiane (she did not die until 1816). Marianne von Willemer enflamed him to a dangerous degree, however, so much so that he was obviously worried about his position *vis-à-vis* her husband, one of his oldest friends; and he was glad that the breaking of a carriage-wheel, as he was about to set off for a third consecutive visit to Frankfurt in 1816, could be used as an omen that the trip should not be made. Yet, as later poems show, he never forgot his promise to Marianne to think of her whenever he saw the full moon, and he wrote her a heart-broken letter when returning her letters in 1831, just before his death.

But this was not all. In 1823 – at the age of 74 – he met and fell in love with Ulrike von Levetzow. And he asked for her hand in marriage, and would have married her (and she him). But her mother felt that the disparity in age was too great, and refused consent (Ulrike was only 19). It was this setback which caused Goethe to write the 'Trilogie der Leidenschaft', including, above all, the great elegy which takes its name from Marienbad, the summer resort where this belated idyll had its birth and death. There is bitter irony in the fact that Ulrike never married, and died at a great age at the end of last century: her gentle love might have prolonged the poet's life even more. She could not, as Goethe's widow, have proved a more unhelpful custodian of Goethe's house and the archives than the ill-starred sons of August were to become.

Of all the emotional entanglements which mark Goethe's last quarter-century none was more productive than his love for Marianne. One reason for this was that unlike most of Goethe's other loves, Marianne was herself a creative writer. She was altogether an unusual person. Austrian by birth, after an unhappy childhood she had become an actress, and was discovered in a company visiting Frankfurt by the art-loving businessman J. J. von Willemer. He found her promise so remarkable that he suggested adopting her as a companion for his own two motherless daughters, who were of more or less her age. After some hesitation she agreed, for life in the moneyed house in Frankfurt was gay and pleasant. Goethe's arrival – he had known about Willemer all his life though this was their first meeting – merely added one more subject of interest for the household. But on Goethe's return visit the following year, what had simply been a charming friendship took on deeper colours: Marianne and the poet came very close to each other over Goethe's new involvement in writing what was to turn into the *Westöstlicher Divan.* A number of the poems in at least one of its books came from Marianne's pen and in one case we can compare her original with what Goethe made of it: the amount of rewriting is small indeed.

The *Westöstlicher Divan*, written over these years but published only in 1819 (according to the dedication of the original, as the poet's 'gift to his own people' – *die Seinen*, meaning his friends and family rather than the Germans as a whole), is the fruit of a number of developments which are important in any view of Goethe's life in the 1810s. Goethe had always been acquainted with the fact that the Orientals wrote poetry but he had not studied any Eastern poetry closely until Josef von Hammer-Purgstall, professor of Eastern Languages at the university of Vienna, published his translation of the early Persian poet Hafiz in 1813. At first Goethe approached Hafiz just as he had used the new ('Romantic') vogue for exotica: the stresses of Napoleon's last years made the poet turn for consolation to a wide range of opiate reading, travel books and books dealing with new experiences such as he had not interested himself in previously. One result of the Schlegel brothers' critical championing of exotic literatures had been a great burst of enthusiasm for a brightening and broadening of the range of the German poets' palette. A concomitant result – arising from the personal interests of Friedrich Schlegel himself – was a great outburst of scholarly interest in languages and literatures beyond the routine study of contemporary universities (that is, Latin and Greek). Despite his position as one of the pundits of contemporary literature, Friedrich Schlegel ultimately spent most of his own time in the foundation of the new science of philology. Many other young scholars, however, who took up Oriental languages in a scientific spirit, finished up, like Hammer-Purgstall, by executing authoritative translations of Oriental literatures (one thinks of Edward FitzGerald's more or less contemporary version of Omar Khayyam).

Goethe was not interested only in the sensuous possibilities of the new literature thus opened up to him. He was attracted by the undogmatic wisdom of the Persian poet. Many of the ideas he came across were in harmony with Gnostic and Orphic ideas in which he was steeping his sorrows – personal disappointments at the gradual decay of his marriage with Christiane; philosophical disappointments, as he sadly observed the cancer of narrow nationalism eating into the minds of young intellectuals as a result of French oppression, and as he saw the beginnings of a cloudy academic idealism settle over university chairs of Philosophy where once the incisive ideas of Leibniz and Kant had reigned; and poetic disappointments, as the first decade of the eighteenth century showed the public's positive acceptance of the childish nonsense which made up so much of the Romantic beginners' work – fairy-tales and sickly romances. For Goethe poetry was becoming more and more a vehicle through which real wisdom could be passed on. As he matured – and, for the moment, in a rather loveless atmosphere – his work became more abstruse. The first decade of the century saw some of Goethe's most thoughtful work – the 'little magazine', *Die Propyläen*, containing some intricate theoretical essays; *Die natürliche Tochter*; *Pandora* (an almost unreadably learned Classical fragment, obviously unfinishable); the Prologue to *Faust Part One*; the complete version of the acute but wrongheaded *Farbenlehre*; and the strangely fascinating but bloodless novel *Die Wahlverwandtschaften*.

Some critics choose to see in this last work the erotic fantasies of a dirty old man. Certainly there is an erotic edge to much of the lyric poetry of this period, such as 'Die Braut von Korinth' and 'Der Gott und die Bajadere', to name only two of the most successful works. Leonard Forster[47] puts a good face on it when he writes: 'Continued protest against Procrustean doctrinalism and fig-leaf squeamishness was an essential feature of Goethe's religious development.' Perhaps, *pace* Mary Wilkinson,[48] the most dubious product is 'Das Tagebuch' (written in 1808 or 1810), which has been said to 'reveal the power of Goethe's art to transform potentially scabrous themes into something human, subtle and delicate'. This poem is based on the story of a traveller who, offered with sensuous frankness a night with a serving-wench in a country inn, finds himself impotent when he thinks of his wife at home. With the best will in the world, one still finds oneself feeling that the Goethe of these years was mentally not entirely healthy.

Then came contact with Hafiz, a desire to write in the Persian vein about the events of the day, and, finally, the new love for the dazzling Marianne. Marianne is not, as many expositions would seem to suggest, the centre of *Westöstlicher Divan*, nor is the collection a conscious attempt to re-create Oriental-type poems: indeed Goethe gets a good deal of ironical effect out of using Oriental rhythms with Greek allusions and vice versa. What Goethe found in Hafiz above all was the Persian willingness to bring the lowest as well as the highest into lyrical expression, a mixture of what Erich Auerbach[49] calls the 'creatural' with the 'intellectual' and which is for this critic one of the central contents of poetry-as-humanism. Marianne helped to bring about this synthesis, though, in addition to the 'Buch der Suleika' which is dedicated to her, there were eleven other books in the collection – and the central 'Buch des Timur' (never, significantly enough, completely finished) was to be dedicated to the shadow of Napoleon.

Use of Oriental forms for cultural criticism had become an intellectual fashion in the eighteenth century: we recall Vol-

[47] L. W. Forster, Introduction to the Penguin Book of German Verse, originally printed London 1957.

[48] Prof. Wilkinson has lectured on this so very often that one will be grateful when she publishes her views in permanent form, so that one may contradict her *expressis verbis*!

[49] E. Auerbach, *Mimesis* (2nd edn Berne 1959).

taire's 'Oriental' tragedies, Montesquieu's use of a Persian and Goldsmith's of a Chinese as critics of Western social life. Herder discussed with Goethe many times his sense of the Bible as a work of Oriental poetry; indeed in this field Goethe undoubtedly saw the Eastern poets as creative figures with the particular advantage of being liberated from a doctrinal religious commitment. So much becomes clear from the *Notes* to the *Divan* which Goethe published with them; they are less clear in themselves than the lyrics, though they form an interesting addition to the literature demonstrating the poet's intellectual interests at the time. The two may well be connected even more closely, if we follow a recent Soviet interpretation of the *Divan* as continuing the Persian tradition of masking political and social criticism under lyrical fancy dress. Certainly Braginski[50] makes out a good case for the few actual poems he interprets, notably the first poem of the introductory 'Buch des Sängers', the 'Hegire', which he interprets as Goethe using the symbol of Mohammed's flight from Mecca as an objective correlative for the position of the Poet in a reactionary world. Indeed, linking 'Hegire' with the concluding poem 'Einlaß' from the final 'Buch des Paradieses', Braginski points stimulatingly to the likeness to *Faust*.

Faust is indeed central to any consideration of Goethe's mature work and is certainly the vital element in his thinking at this period. 1800 was, interestingly enough, the year in which the poet finally decided that he could not carry out his original intentions within the confines of one single play and would need to divide the play into two. But it was, even more strikingly, the year in which he planned and sketched the first version of the third act of this second part, the central station in Faust's progress, the act in which he meets, woos, wins and lives happily but ultimately fruitlessly with Helen of Troy, the so-called *'Helena-Akt'*. This act marks a stage in Goethe's intellectual development towards his last period. It was actually finished separately, before the final completion of the work, and published as the fourth volume of the final edition of the poet's works, the *Ausgabe letzter Hand*, which the publisher Cotta produced in 1826.

[50] J. S. Braginski, 'Die West-östliche Synthese im "Divan" Goethes' in *Weimarer Beiträge*, Vol. 2 (1968).

Because, then, of the significance of *Faust* in Goethe's intellectual growth, we must now turn to an inspection of the poet's relation to the subject, and its various metamorphoses over the years.

Chapter 11

Faustian Problems

Faust was, in the first place, a kind of historical drama. As such, we may suggest that the subject of the old chap-book appealed to Goethe in the same way that the folk-songs he collected around Strasbourg moved him, as a disciple of Herder. In the folk-songs Goethe thought he saw the artless beauty of 'natural' products unaffected by the over-sophistication of what he considered to be 'modern life' (*we* might think of it as 'French taste of the rococo sort'). In the Faust chap-book Goethe thought he saw the artless philosophy of earlier centuries when Germany was more itself – that is, before it had been submerged by the taste for the rococo. In his mind it was doubtless no more a historical drama than was *Götz*: in their so-called 'return to the Middle Ages' (actually a return to the German Renaissance), Herder and Goethe were essentially stressing their opposition to the fashionable dictates of pseudo-Versailles culture, consciously or unconsciously polemizing against the absolutism of their time.

E. M. Butler[51] investigated many sides of the Faust legend. She underlined the popularity of the myth of the Magus, giving examples from many periods, from the New Testament Apollonius of Tyre up to charismatic faith-healers of our own century, such as Mary Baker Eddy and Madame Blavatsky. It was this side of Faust that impressed Goethe's followers and imitators as late as Thomas Mann, whose demonic composer Adrian Leverkühn symbolizes the cultured Wilhelmine Germany seduced into throwing itself into the arms of the Nazis. But it held little attrac-

[51] E. M. Butler, *The Myth of the Magus* (Cambridge 1948) and *The Fortunes of Faust* (Cambridge 1952). I hope that this book will please the shade of Elsie Butler, wherever it is now resting.

tion for Goethe. There is little historical mumbo-jumbo about his treatment of the Faust theme, either in the original or in the final part. As we shall see, not a little of the popularity of the tragedy, certainly as performed on the stage, is due to the fact that Goethe's devil, Mephistopheles, smacks so little of fire and brimstone, and is so civilized and urbane.

Yet Goethe did exercise a great influence on modern literary trends by choosing to use the sixteenth-century chap-book. This curious product, one of the most fateful of Germany's contributions to the European literary scene, was written in the last third of the sixteenth century and first published, as far as we know, in Frankfurt. It purported, like many early broadsheets and ballads, to be a true account of the life of one of the humanists of the first half of the century, Dr Johannes or Georgius Faust. There is some documentary evidence on this scholar and also a little contemporary gossip to the effect that he was either a confidence-trickster or a dabbler in black magic or both. None of this was at all unusual for an academic during the Renaissance period. Indeed, as a black magician Faust would have been in the company of distinguished scholars like the Frenchman Nostradamus, the Swiss Paracelsus and his own fellow-countryman Agrippa von Nettesheim. In each case it is difficult to disentangle the boundaries between real scholarship and mumbo-jumbo. After all, the roots of chemistry and alchemy are not only philologically in the same place: Priestley wrote as many allegorical books as he did descriptions of the periodic table; Newton was as keen on cabbalistic theology as on astronomy; and so on. . . .

The reason why Faust was chosen to be the subject of the chap-book is possibly precisely his obscurity. Snide attacks on Nettesheim or Paracelsus might have brought to their defence the kind of humanistic united front which had earlier in the century sprung to the defence of Johannes Reuchlin when he was attacked by the Dominicans of Cologne (the *Epistolae obscurorum virorum*). But no one probably bothered about the person of Faust and so he could be held up to the semi-illiterate public which bought chap-books in the fairs and markets as the model of one of those foolish scholars whose useless learning merely led him into rejection of the True Faith. Popular preachers have been attacking university scholars on these grounds for the last six hundred years. The list of victims of the 'revivalist preacher' starts at Peter Abelard and continues through to Robert J. Oppenheimer, Eduard Goldstücker and Bertrand Russell. Doubtless most people no longer consider these men as undertaking pacts with the Devil; but naïve minds can undoubtedly be led to think of them as having been led off some divinely ordained 'correct' path on to some equally ordained path of wickedness.

Though Faust was chosen as the subject of a work of fancy and treated in a traditional manner within a German setting, the scope of the story at once struck home outside Germany. Within a few years of the book's first printing, Christopher Marlowe had taken it up and turned it into a tragedy. The story of the book's transit to England is mysterious and, of course, the heterodox Marlowe was probably as much attracted to the black magician as repelled by him. But this drama is not amongst Marlowe's best compositions. The story was powerful enough, however, to take its place amongst the dramas which the very many English Elizabethan actors touring the Reich brought with them – together with many plays of Shakespeare and the melodramas of the Jacobeans. This hardly elevated the tone of the German stage but it made the theatre one of the most popular entertainments throughout the length and breadth of the Reich. For Goethe the significant thing is that in the 1750s his grandmother presented him with a puppet-theatre, and the story of Faust was one of the scenarios that went with it. It is not unusual for theatre repertoire to be a century out of date: the Pollock theatres which children buy today are still equipped with century-old Victorian melodramas. There is also some likelihood that he could have seen an actual performance of the play by a strolling troupe which visited Frankfurt during his childhood.

The young beau who visited Auerbach's Cellar during his years at the university of Leipzig might indeed have had a mild *frisson* at the thought of what these precincts were, and he may have felt a suspicion of diabolism in the sophistication of his mentor Behrisch; yet it is unlikely that he would have felt impelled to dramatize the story, except, as is always possible, as an undergraduate satire on the aridity of the academic curriculum in the university. His main dramatic efforts at this time were strictly 'Frenchified', comedies of manners *à la* Crébillon.

It was the spirit of Herder which opened his eyes to some of the possibilities of the Faust theme. The idea that Shakespeare was a brother and not a descendant of Sophocles led to the corollary that the ideal German form was, as Lessing had just proclaimed, more likely to be Shakespearian than Sophoclean: subject-matter should be 'national', moreover, and not 'decently' neutralized (that is, in Boileau's manner), or Atticized. The first theme to spring to Goethe's mind was *Götz*, and very faithfully did Goethe give it a Shakespearian treatment. The second theme was undoubtedly *Faust*, though one may surmise that at this stage the poet's plan for a final version (if indeed he ever had one, a suggestion which a contemporary letter of his would seem to discount) will have been more like Thomas Mann's plot than the plot which was to force itself on him in Frankfurt a few years later. The core of the old plot was simply Faust's dissatisfaction with academic life and his useless learning, and the restlessness which was ultimately symbolized in the scene where Faust turned to translate St John's Gospel and could only be satisfied in the first line with the phrase 'In the beginning was *the deed* – not 'the Word'. This dissatisfaction is an expression of Goethe's Sturm und Drang restlessness. He was filled with an immense feeling of his own genius (the critics use the word 'titanism' to express this restless feeling for the disparity between the humdrum world in which he lived and his own giant aspirations) and chose the legend as an objective correlative. Faust seemed to the young Law student to be a man of precisely his stamp, one thoroughly discontented with the limitations imposed on him by his academic environment.

Round this theme Goethe built a number of dramatic episodes. Some are humorously satirical, like the interviews with Wagner – the smug low-grade scholar – and with the student – the naïve outsider who believes in what the Public Relations men of Education tell him. Some are intensely dramatic, for example, Faust's vain attempt to conjure up the Earth Spirit and his curt and painful dismissal by the spirit, which says to him, *'Du gleichst dem Geist/den du begreifst/nicht mir'*. And some are amusingly theatrical, like the scene in Auerbach's Cellar (an obvious choice for the ex-student from Leipzig). These were the scenes which may have been conceived in Leipzig and sketched in Strasbourg, and which were certainly written out on the young graduate's return to his native city.

Here the execution of the child-murderess Susanna Brandt gave him new inspiration for the sexual side of the story. As one would expect from a sixteenth-century story the anonymous chap-book writer provided no sex-interest in the more modern sense. Faust demanded rejuvenation because he wished to have more of his academic life – that is all. He incidentally wanted to see the most beautiful woman in the world and, encountering Helen of Troy, took her as his mistress and lived with her for most of his twenty wicked years. All this is recounted quite dispassionately; the author thought it all self-evident and was sure that his audience would have exactly the same reaction. He spread himself much more on food and on displays of vaudeville magic: here Goethe certainly did not wish to follow him (as indeed he did not follow Marlowe in his idealistic approach to Absolute Beauty). At first he had no more idea of a sex-ridden Faust than Lessing had had in *his* bare outline scenario. Friederike and the alleged murderess changed all that, and Goethe suddenly wanted his rejuvenated Faust to be beset by Sex. In this he succeeded magnificently, both in showing a Faust randy to the point of low comedy, and in showing love-scenes between Faust and Gretchen which were the first in Germany in which modern Romantic love was successfully expressed on the stage.

In all these twists and turns of his fate Faust was accompanied by a Mephistopheles who could well have come from Marlowe – for the chap-book scarcely gave him more than a mention. Marlowe did not do him justice, but he did show that there was some possibility of building a new major character in the devil who had to be Faust's constant tempter-companion: for modern Man scarcely shares the sixteenth-century author's belief that Faust is likely enough to go on deteriorating of his own accord *simply* because he has signed a pact with some abstract personification of evil. The point is taken very nicely by Thomas Mann who produces a bizarrely surrealistic devil to come to terms with his Leverkühn, because in his own twentieth-century surroundings he, for his part, can no longer afford a Mephistopheles. Goethe *could* afford a stage-devil; in his day theories of characterization in the theatre had just about reached a level at which he could (at least in theory – for no actual performances were given until 1829) envisage a Mephistopheles who would be played straight and not like a circus clown.

Mention has already been made of the three early friends whose traits went into the creation of Mephistopheles – the sophomore Behrisch, the worldly *abbé* Herder, and the sardonic Merck. There is, of course, more to Mephistopheles than the sum of all this: at times, as when Goethe splashes on the sombre colours of the obscene Mephistopheles of the Witches' Kitchen and the *Walpurgisnacht*, the result is remarkable: the Goethe who had the normal healthy male's 'dirty' mind does appear all through his life, in many of his conversations, in some of the poems which were suppressed at an earlier period, and in a variety of forms in later creative works. At other times, Goethe describes Mephisto with astonishing acuteness as a kind of very contemporary gangster: this was the 'anticipatory' ability to draw real characters whom he met only years later, about which the poet boasted to later memorialists. Thus there are magnificent moments in the Devil's later scenes, even in the *Urfaust*: his violent reply to the Faust who upbraids him for allowing him to neglect the pregnant Gretchen; his tactical planning of the attempt to liberate her from prison and, finally, the splendid melodrama of his actual role in the final prison scene.

In the second part Mephistopheles still has many roles to play; he is essential for the dynamic movement of the action. But he is no longer as exciting as he was in the beginning. His acid tongue remains, especially when he appears as Phorkyas and helps Faust make the fateful descent to the mysterious Mothers in order to prepare his way to marrying Helen of Troy. He is inventive and urbane at the Imperial court and it is he who invents modern banking for the benefit of the impoverished Emperor: but this is all a clever device. The central role has passed to

Faust, and Mephistopheles has become merely the executant; this is most apparent in the last two acts where he lends his 'aid' to Faust's land-settlement schemes whilst ensuring that the starry-eyed Utopian shall actually be robbed of his final reward, just as he robs him of his peace of mind when he drives Philemon and Baucis to a violent death. The Devil of the final operatic scene has degenerated to being merely a pseudo-*advocatus*: he has entirely lost the splendid panache of his appearance in the Prologue in Heaven.

Goethe did not apparently realize until 1800 that he could not carry out his original intentions in one single play. Until then he had tinkered about with *Urfaust*, adding odd scenes here and there. An obvious sign of this was the decision in 1790 to publish the existing bits and pieces in the collected works: this is the version known as *Faust, Ein Fragment*, and it was the first chance the German public had had of becoming acquainted with what one philosopher, Oswald Spengler, has even called the quintessential image of the modern German *Volk*. The tragedy as it here appears is an expressionist corona of brilliant dramatic moments. The thing the poet had not been able to do was to invent a plausible plot for a properly shaped tragedy: above all he had not yet properly envisaged any way of bringing about the arrival of Mephistopheles, nor had he got over the difficulty of making Faust forget Gretchen for the nine months of her pregnancy.

It was this stretch of time which first became malleable in his hands. In mid-1797 he wrote part of what ultimately became the Walpurgis Night scene. The idea doubtless came to him on one of his various visits to the Harz and his ascents of the wild Brocken hill, with its legends about witches' sabbaths. He had already, by inserting the fatal duel between Faust and Gretchen's brother, Valentine, given an inkling of the fact that something dreadful must have occurred to make Faust need to leave hurriedly without saying farewell to Martha or Gretchen. He exploited this now to pass magically over the months, with the Walpurgis Night revels standing for all the enchantments by means of which the Devil would undoubtedly be trying to divert and ensnare his victim. The need to escape was also cleverly prepared in the witty sparring scenes between Mephistopheles and Martha, where the widow's pressing wooing underlines the Devil's own need to show the earthlings a clean pair of heels. Goethe ultimately prepared the way for the return in a highly imaginative way, using the obscene choreography of the revels to let Faust see a pallid ghost whose features at last remind him of the girl he had deserted. From there Goethe had a clear path back to the wonderful '*Wald und Höhle*' scene which he had begun to add in Italy.

Almost at once the beginnings of the alliance between Faust and his familiar began to fall into place. At the end of the month in which he had started the Walpurgis scenes he began to write the Prologue in Heaven and the scene of the pact between Faust and Mephistopheles. But the whole of the machinery of those scenes, in which the Devil circles more and more closely round his victim until he can finally materialize from a poodle into a creature of apparent flesh and blood, was not completely worked out until April 1804; the final version of '*Faust Part One*' did not appear with Cotta until 1808. A great deal had to be added to the original version in order to bring about the meeting of the two characters: one highly interesting scene was the Easter Walk, and, following on this, the scenes in which the poodle actually turns into the Devil – a clumsy sequence which can scarcely have been easy to produce until modern stagecraft both made the physical presence of a dog unnecessary, and provided lighting devices suitable to engineering a really impressive entry for Mephistopheles.

The Easter Walk – involving Faust in deep conversation about his role in society, even though his interlocutor is the hopelessly narrow-minded Wagner – was a neat thematic development of the original scene in which Faust's suicide was prevented by the irruption of a burst of Easter music from the university church, giving the despairing Faust at least *some* thought about resurrection and salvation. At the time when he wrote the *Urfaust*, the immediate snatch of action which followed this in the poet's mind was Faust's turning to his translation of St John's Gospel, enabling the author to muse aloud once more on the philosophical scepticism besetting his hero. Now the same events gave him purely structural material – the walk itself, which illuminated further sides of Faust's character (though the development of these made a second part ultimately inevitable); the encounter with the poodle and its transformation into a disguised Mephisto; and the atmospheric and amusing peripeteia of Faust's gradual submission to the Devil.

By this time Goethe had realized the imperative necessity of having two parts, and his collaboration with Schiller in the practical work of the Weimar Theatre had given him assurance that two-part tragedy was viable and had indeed already been planned by his collaborator (in the case of his double-barrelled *Wallenstein*). At once he set about drafting two of the major episodes of the second part, the grand central Act III in which Faust woos and wins Helen of Troy, and the final scene showing the hero's redemption (merely indicated at the end of Part One by a voice from on high crying *'Ist gerettet'*.

But an enormous hiatus now ensues. The aftermath of the Napoleonic Wars, the vast business of coming to terms with the Romantic poets, and the onset of a completely new world after 1815, which drove Goethe more and more into study of the natural sciences, all conspired to make work on any elaboration of a creative poetic work of the magnitude of *Faust* seem nothing more than a pipe-dream. Finally, in the early 1820s, the publisher Cotta suggested to the now septuagenarian Goethe the production of a definitive edition of his works the *Ausgabe letzter Hand*. This was to be much more complete than any previous edition and the old man was forced to realize that this was not something which he could do entirely on his own. He was by no means without friends in his beloved Weimar but it was difficult to envisage any of them as literary secretaries in this sense. The most likely one would have been the librarian F. W. Riemer, but even he was a court official, besides being perhaps somewhat too pompous for comfortable collaboration. Goethe turned accordingly to the idea of employing some young man who had displayed interest in him, hovered for some time between two schoolmasters who had written perceptive books about aspects of his work, and finally settled – almost accidentally – for a third young man, J. P. Eckermann, a young, almost self-educated and penniless Hamburger, who had written a good essay on the poet's work, sent it to him for approval and recommendation to a publisher, and then followed it up with a personal visit, for which he walked all the way from the north.[52]

Eckermann, despite the persistent rumour to this effect, was never Goethe's secretary in the sense of being paid to write letters.

Goethe retained him at first for doing specific editorial jobs from month to month: for this he had him paid by Cotta. Then he persuaded the young man that it would be good for his education to stay in Weimar, and obtained from others tutoring and teaching jobs for him (this largely involved instructing young Englishmen in German). Finally he obtained a small court sinecure for him, and so Eckermann remained for good, the last important recruit to the Weimar 'Musenhof'. All this happened while he was reading and working himself into Goethe's vast corpus of work. In the course of the intensive editorial work, the subject of *Faust* was constantly raised, and Eckermann developed what Goethe in a most generous tribute later called his 'remarkable faculty of squeezing and teasing fresh work out of him', until on 22 July 1831 the whole of *Faust Part Two* was finally completed and parcelled up. Only after Goethe's death, in fact, was it opened and edited as the first volume of the posthumous works by Eckermann and Riemer, in their fateful roles as Goethe's literary executors.

In 1825 work was centred on the first and last acts. Then Act III, the one planned earlier, was carried out in great detail; it was written with so much love that Goethe almost thought of it as a new work and published it separately in 1826 as the fourth volume of the *Ausgabe letzter Hand.* Act II grew out of the work on Act I, of which it is essentially a completion, though Goethe began in it the necessary preparations for the magical hocus-pocus which enables Faust to conjure up a corporeal Helen of Troy. For this purpose he returned to some of the ideas of Part One and set the scene in the study in which Part One began, which is now occupied by Wagner, no less an insensitive

[52] See my 'On correcting Eckermann's perspectives', *Proc. Eng. Goethe Soc.*, Vol. XXIII (1955), pp. 1–26.

figure of fun for having become a professor – Faust's successor, indeed – and a scientist who is experimenting on the production of human life in a test-tube. This modern-sounding idea is, however, merely used to provide a means by which Mephisto can enable Faust to penetrate to the Mothers and thus win his Helen.

Act III was described by Goethe as a 'romantic-classical phantasmagoria' and, indeed, much literary art was lavished on a skilful blending of the two cultures which haunted Goethe all his life, the Gothic world of the north and the essentially extrovert world of the south.[53] One notable device is the skilful way in which Helen and her handmaidens are taught to speak in rhyme as opposed to the numbered Classical metres to which they are accustomed. There are innumerable loose ends into which it is impossible to inquire too deeply; the essential thing is the impression which the audience gains of Faust's high endeavour in wooing Helen, the joy of their married life, and the inevitable tragedy which ensues, since in the end it is impossible for Man simply to re-create past worlds and live off them. Goethe linked this existential tragedy with the ultimate death of Euphorion, the young son of Faust and Helen (a tribute from the poet to Byron, whom he admired warmly, and with whom he was personally linked in a bizarre indirect fashion before the Englishman's untimely death at Missolonghi). Like Byron Euphorion was, says Goethe, too splendid to last in a materialistic environment. With his death, however, the whole Classical dream began to dissolve and Faust was left once more unsatisfied.

Goethe already knew that he wanted Faust to be redeemed. He now set about displaying this redemption. If the final scenes of the drama are more operatic than dramatic and so symbolical as to be deeply obscure, this is partly the result of Goethe's great age and partly an inevitable outcome of even the most skilfully planned modern Utopia. What is most interesting about the last scenes is the way in which the poet introduced split-level stage effects, derived from his recent study of the Pre-Raphaelite painters; his use of devices to indicate dreams, suggested to him by Mozart's *Magic Flute*, which so impressed him that he went

[53] See Forster, 'Lynkeus' Masque in Faust II', *German Life and Letters*, Vol. XXIII (1970), No. 1, pp. 62–70.

as far as to write a libretto for a continuation;[54] and the pervasive permeation of the whole by a Catholicizing mysticism which is wholly surprising in one who was very far from approving the Catholicizing tendencies so prevalent in the ideology of the time. Is this because so much of Western art is bound up with the Roman Church that it is almost impossible, for instance, to think of oratorio without thinking of church masses, or of adulatory painting without thinking of the art of the Counter-Reformation? In this sense it was impossible for Goethe to provide a counterpart to the Prologue in Heaven which would not ultimately sound like the final transformation scene of a Calderon mystery-play.

Finally the poet set about his fourth act. This raised peculiar difficulties since it was to depict Faust's final transformation from mystical dreamer to practical man. Goethe knew that this was what he wanted, but it was difficult for him to achieve it in a way which would maintain the elevated poetical level to which the tragedy had attained up to this point. Goethe's solution was to show Faust's intervention in an Imperial civil war and his vast reward, limitless coastland for reclamation. A sinister but symbolically highly important episode is Mephisto's expropriation of Philemon and Baucis, whose tiny cottage prevents Faust having unlimited access to his new property. The implications of this – that great undertakings planned by Utopians are always likely to be carried out crudely by less idealistic underlings – are then stressed as Mephisto summons his myrmidons, in an impressively solemn scene, to undermine Faust's physical well-being. Gone is the Devil's assurance that Faust will lose his wager through an excess of self-confidence. Unlike Marlowe, moreover, Goethe did not insist on a time-limit for the wager, realizing that this is comparatively unimportant within his framework – Thomas Mann, on the other hand, could return to a time-limit because his aim was to satirize the Thousand-Year Reich, which lasted only twelve years. Hell now brings forward its crudest weapons. One of these, Care, blinds the hero. The philosophical tables have been turned: Faust is no longer the unthinking

[54] Samuel, op. cit. (n. 30).

wrecker of Part One; he has become a far-seeing Utopian. So Providence robs him of the joy of watching his work being fulfilled. Mephisto exploits this to sabotage his orders; Faust dies ultimately, satisfied at the sound of what he thinks are free men digging on the free land he has obtained for them. In fact what he is hearing are Mephisto's lemurs digging his grave.

It was an ingenious and a thoroughly honest solution. The final scenes were retained because dramatic symmetry demanded them. From the standpoint of the allegory they were no longer necessary. In fact, the reminder of Gretchen at the end now seems a very vague remembrance of things past and the final '*Das Ewig-Weibliche zieht uns hinan*' otiose. But it was perhaps the fact that this ending offered so much scope for hazy minds that commended it to posterity. German scholars surpassed themselves in interpreting it. Finally Spengler made Faust into one of the foundation-stones of his interpretation of modern civilization. Guilt by association with Nazism has thus brought *Faust* into some discredit: the Mephisto of the Prologue in Heaven was, as a civilized Enlightenment gentleman, unlikely to have welcomed seeing himself as a relation of *Parteigenosse* Faustian Man, the volunteer member of the S.S. Cavalry Corps! Doubtless it was Mephisto's urbane wit which designed the somewhat less than grand final scenes of the Thousand-Year Reich, with their mutual recriminations, squalid suicides, and furtive evasions.

Despite this, performances of the whole of *Faust* have formed some of the most significant theatrical events of the post-war years.

Chapter 12

Life in Victorian Weimar

In one sense it may be said that there were three separate sides to Goethe in the last three decades of his life – and especially after the death of Christiane in 1816. There was Goethe the family man, the *Familienvater*, as lumpishly playful, first with the banal Christiane and later with his daughter-in-law Ottilie and her offspring, as any pompous, well-known German playing at being the *Familienvater*. There was the 'Geheimrat' (as he was angrily called by those who were either offended or amused by the pose), cold and dignified, remarkably taciturn until the right psychological stimulus was applied. And finally there was Goethe the writer, accessible only fitfully to his circle in Weimar but always revealed in his vast correspondence and, of course, in the works which he produced.

To recite the course of Goethe's life in these last thirty-two years is not terribly profitable. He spent most of his time in Weimar, meditating, writing, entertaining and being entertained, and carrying out a strikingly large programme of public activity as *de facto* Minister for the Arts in the government of the duchy. He was, of course, one of the 'sights' of literary Europe, and so everybody came to him. Those who did not visit Weimar in person – and a surprisingly large number of Eastern European intellectuals, particularly, made the long journey – corresponded with him. In this way he was in touch with Byron and Manzoni, Walter Scott and Ampère – in fact, with almost all the leading figures of the Romantic movement of the 1810s and 1820s.

The work which he carried out for his old friend Karl August (who did not die until 1828) kept him busy travelling around the little state; and since communications were still primitive, these little journeys represented important upheavals. Eckermann has left us what are probably accurate descriptions of one or two of these formal visits of inspection: there was, for instance, a fortnight's stay in Jena where Goethe, as official Visitor to the university, had to inspect the library, a job which he carried out methodically and painstakingly, though, of course, the visit also allowed him more personal diversions, such as a visit to Schiller's old house and an evening of reminiscence with his old colleague and friend Knebel. Nor were these journeys always as innocent as they seemed. From 1802 to 1808 Goethe was involved in a passionate sentimental attachment to Silvie von Ziegesar, the daughter of a landowner with an estate close to Jena who served as an administrator at the nearby court of Gotha. The Ziegesar family were friendly with a number of Goethe's Jena friends, in particular, the circle of the bookseller and printer Fromann. There were thus ample opportunities for the two to meet in Jena, and they frequently did so; what is more, these friendly encounters were extended in the summer when both Goethe and the Ziegesars spent holidays in the Bohemian mountains. The course of the affair was not by any means straight, and it was crossed violently at one stage in 1807 by a fleeting bout of calf-love on the part of the poet for the even younger Wilhelmina (Minna) Herzlieb, Fromann's adopted daughter.[55]

The points of interest about this sentimental attachment are, first, how little it interrupted Goethe's family life with Christiane (whom he eventually married in 1806 in order to repay her for her steadfastness in the face of insults from the occupying French soldiery). Intellectually they had nothing in common, but this was probably unimportant. Her role was to minister to his physical needs, and in his domestic life Goethe appears as the galumphing intellectual German, relaxed and comical. The sight is often faintly nauseating: the intimate correspondence between Goethe and Christiane is as inane as any such correspondence

[55] Most of Wolff's second book (*Goethe in der Periode der Wahlverwandschaften*) is devoted to elucidating the story of Silvie. There is a vast literature on Goethe's relations with women which only adds usable historical facts here and there.

is likely to be, though it is startling at times in the insights it gives into some of Goethe's sexual fetichisms and the domestic perversions practised at the time!

The second point of interest about Goethe's relationship with Silvie is, however, the astonishingly high level of sensuousness at which the whole (essentially innocent) flirtation was conducted. The Ziegesar family were pious Lutheran aristocrats; they formed a devoted and tightly-knit group. Yet Goethe was warmly welcomed into their midst at all times and no one ever seems to have raised an eyebrow at the fact that there was more than ordinary affection between him and their daughter, who was some forty years his junior. Not even a family friend like the genteel portrait-painter Luise Seidler, one of Silvie's closest friends, passed any judgement on the highly emotional scenes which she described in detail in her diary. It must be remembered, of course, that the eighteenth century was an age of sentimentality just as much as an age of reason, and that the element of sentimentality was carried over, sometimes in a highly exaggerated form, into the Romantic age of the first decades of the nineteenth century. It can therefore be assumed that the respectable Ziegesars were not outraged to see their grown-up daughter welcome the famous poet by flinging her arms round his neck and bursting into tears on his shoulder. The diary of Goethe's life in the company of the Ziegesars during their holiday weeks in Marienbad or Franzensbad includes simple family romps, charades and musical soirées, walks in the moonlight, and much reading of lyrical verse. All these activities, which raised Goethe's sexual passions to a pitch of excitement easily sensed in the literary works which show the influence of these years, affected the Ziegesars hardly at all; certainly no one made any finger-wagging comment when shortly after Goethe loosened the magnetic links which had bound him to Silvie – in 1809 – she became engaged to a respectable Lutheran pastor. When she married him, she devotedly shared the not inconsiderable poverty which he had to undergo when he voluntarily left his university post for a parish; ultimately he became the superintendent (bishop, in Anglican terms) of a minor Saxon duchy.

One oddity about Goethe's attachment to Silvie von Ziegesar

is the fact that because the information which does exist about the relationship is so scattered, and because there was little malicious gossip about it at the time, it has often been ignored by those biographers of Goethe who otherwise have revelled in writing lyrically about the more highly-coloured friendships of Germany's greatest poet. And indeed as a source of inspiration for Goethe's lyrical verse Silvie cannot be put into the same category as, for instance, Marianne von Willemer. She did, however, play an important role in his work on the stories which make up *Wilhelm Meisters Wanderjahre*; she is probably the crucial figure in his inspiration for *Wahlverwandtschaften*; and it is likely that the heart-searchings which the affair caused Goethe inspired him to start work on his autobiography, *Dichtung und Wahrheit*. Since none of these works counts amongst the more popular of the poet's writings one can understand the process by which Silvie's name came to be omitted from the canon of Goethe's muses. The most striking lyrical production of these years, moreover, which probably is connected with Silvie, underwent a curious transformation at the last moment. Goethe's lightning infatuation with the teenage Minna Herzlieb, Fromann's foster-daughter, caused the insertion of a direct reference to her into one of the *Sonette* of 1807, which led most subsequent critics to assume that it was this mouse-like child who was the inspiration for a series of passionate poems. From a literary point of view, these poems also owe a considerable debt to Goethe's passing friendship with one of the more eccentric Romantic writers, Zacharias Werner, who was visiting Jena at the time. Werner was a mystic with a tendency to guru-like behaviour; his personal flashiness and inclinations to Roman Catholicism would under other circumstances not have recommended him to Geheimrat von Goethe. But in 1807 Goethe was in a highly emotional frame of mind; Werner more or less challenged him to the production of this sonnet sequence otherwise the artificial sonnet form was not one which normally recommended itself to Goethe.

Despite the onset of this emotional crisis in the middle years of the first decade of the century Goethe ultimately recovered his self-control: his passion for Silvie, like his crush on Minna, passed away without after-taste. It is probable that 'Das Tagebuch', an erotic poem usually thought to date from 1810, was written in 1808, and that the suggestion that it is faithfulness to his lawful wife which renders the wayward husband incapable of making love to a serving-wench symbolizes Goethe's final determination to keep intact the bond now uniting him legally to Christiane. Nevertheless, the very fact that 'Das Tagebuch' is an erotic poem does underline a great change in the poet's *Weltanschauung* brought about by this period.

Goethe's attitude to the sensual aspect of life ebbed and flowed during the course of his long career. Thus he swung from a gay and irresponsible cult of the 'genius' in his Sturm und Drang period – the mood in which his Egmont made no bones about living 'in sin' with Klärchen – to a period of platonic reserve under the influence of Charlotte von Stein during his first ten years in Weimar. This self-restraint undoubtedly was a strain and it was thrown off for a mood of irresponsible sensualism during his stay in Italy and during the years when he first took Christiane to live in his house. But the shocks following the outbreak of the French Revolution and his contact with the reserved Schiller household brought on a desire for withdrawal from the sensual world, a feeling which was uppermost in his mind at the turn of the century and which is strikingly reflected in the rarified atmosphere of *Die natürliche Tochter*. This was the mood of the poet at the time when he met Silvie, and we can trace in the works which flowed from his pen during this period the stages by which he gradually surfaced from his renewed immersion in the waters of Schillerian Platonism. The transition was all the more painful since it is obvious that Fräulein von Ziegesar was not a powerful personality and, above all, was much more sentimental than sensual. It is essentially a reflection on the atmosphere of these Romantic years that Goethe should have been able to extract so strong a personal sexual reaction from a friendship which, in its external course, was entirely a matter of emotionally charged walks, fireside poetry readings and sentimental exchanges of tokens and notes.

How violent the sexual passions unlocked in the poet were is clear, above all, from their reflection in the novel *Die Wahlverwandtschaften*, written in 1808. The story, the infatuation of a middle-aged man for a young girl, reflects exactly the situation in which Goethe found himself, and was foreshadowed by a number of the short stories inserted into the final version of *Wilhelm Meister*, the *Wanderjahre*. Goethe received the initial inspiration for 'Der Mann von 50 Jahren' in 1803, though the bulk of the writing was not carried out until 1807. The story was re-planned in 1808, its first chapter published in 1816 and the final version written – under the inspiration this time of Ulrike von Levetzow – in 1826–7. There are also reflections on love between people of different ages and on unhappy marriages in 'Die neue Melusine', which moves in feeling from Sturm und Drang passion to sheer heart-broken resignation between its conception in 1797 and its completion in 1807. The idea for 'Das nußbraune Mädchen', another story of star-crossed love over barriers, also first came to Goethe in 1807; the story took years to complete, and was in an incomplete form in 1815 before it was finally finished in 1824–5.

These stories (and others which have echoes of Goethe's problem, like 'St Joseph der Zweite' and 'Die gefährliche Wette' were sketches such as Goethe the pictorial artist was liable to dash off when confronted with romantic scenery. For the full working out of Goethe's problem we must turn to *Die Wahlverwandtschaften*. Here too we are confronted with a change of intention on the part of the author : there is reason to believe that the final version of the novel was almost doubled in length by the insertion of a central portion which resulted in taking the blame off the hero and pushing it almost imperceptibly on to the shoulders of his wife.[56] This can be said to mirror Goethe's own fluctuations of mood during the Silvie period, from the resigned mood of *Die natürliche Tochter* to the more dynamic and sensual mood into which he then moved. In this mood, only a few years later, he was to be capable of enjoying with complete abandon his flirta-

[56] The growing literature on *Wahlverwandtschaften* needs careful handling. H. G. Barnes' *Goethe's Die Wahlverwandtschaften* (Oxford 1967) is thorough but often unperceptive. Wolff, op. cit., is most concerned with disentangling what he considers the various strata of the plot. Some very acute judgements are found in W. Benjamin, *Goethes Wahlverwandtschaften*, readily available as an Insel pocket-book (Frankfurt 1955).

tion with Marianne, which resulted in an outpouring of vital lyrical poetry inspired by his newly found happiness.

The novel is the story of a middle-aged couple, Eduard and Charlotte. They had been childhood sweethearts but were separated by adverse circumstances, and both had undergone loveless marriages from which they had emerged to enter on a happy union. This is disturbed, as the novel opens, by the arrival of a young girl, Ottilie, Eduard's god-daughter. It would seem that in the original version Eduard falls in love with Ottilie by gradual stages, ultimately seduces her and is saved from divorce only by Ottilie's sudden remorse, which sends her into a decline ending in her death. This version was written in 1808 under the immediate impact of Goethe's dying but still painful passion for Silvie. After he had worked Silvie out of his system, he no longer felt such overwhelming guilt, and in 1809 inserted an almost completely new series of incidents into the original plot, during the course of which Eduard joins a foreign army engaged on a military campaign. The most astonishing element added during this final revision is, however, that Charlotte is also tempted to leave the path of marital virtue, falling in love with a middle-aged friend of the family, a cultured bachelor captain. Nor is this all. During Eduard's absence Ottilie continues to live in Charlotte's house and devotes herself to serving Charlotte and her child. But a recrudescence of Ottilie's emotional disturbance makes her neglect the baby, which drowns; guilt so preys on her mind that she dies. In this new version, it will be seen, Charlotte is almost as much at fault as Eduard, whilst Ottilie's death has a much more concrete cause; less is now heard of personal responsibility for extra-marital infidelity.

This novel is filled to the brim with damagingly repressed sexuality, which gives it a strangely modern aspect; so much so that some critics have called it the erotic fantasy of an old man. Looked at in the light of Goethe's struggle for self-control in the first decade of the nineteenth century, however, it can be seen as a remarkable testimony to a great internal convulsion. When one considers, for example, the many social obligations which Geheimrat von Goethe was carrying out at the time of his crisis, the necessity for the stiff Geheimrat façade becomes eminently understandable. But there is also the evidence of the poet's letters to Christiane to show that there were moments of reconciliation with her which led to a complete emotional liberation – even though it is in these moments that the Olympian Goethe becomes a predictable member of the great middle class with very bourgeois personal habits.

It was the purged Goethe, prepared to accept flights of emotion as nothing terribly sinful or damaging, who spent two delightful summers in 1814 and 1815 with the Willemers in Frankfurt. The hedonist even took some quite bourgeois precautions to ensure that Christiane did not have to add Marianne to the list of 'scarlet women' with whom she would reproach him during the inevitable marital quarrels (this list included, by the way, both Silvie and Minna, apart from many more who were simply sentimental devotees of the poet's). But even so Goethe was prepared to believe that enough was enough and to accept the breaking of a carriage wheel in 1816 as a sign that he should not go to Frankfurt for yet a third summer. 1816 was a crucial year in many respects. Christiane died and with her Goethe's last emotions as a bourgeois husband. It is true that his feelings did not dry up completely: he enjoyed a mild Indian summer in the 1820s in the midst of August's and his daughter-in-law's growing family and was even moved to propose marriage in 1824 to the very young Ulrike von Levetzow. But the Geheimrat pose had become fixed; his defences were seldom lowered for any outsider in the last decade of his life.

For this we have one of the most remarkable testimonies that any great man ever had, the delightful *Gespräche mit Goethe in den letzten Jahren seines Lebens*, written by the young Johann Peter Eckermann, who came to Weimar in 1823 and was retained as literary amanuensis.[57] After the First World War a pompous nationalistic academic pundit in Berlin tried to discredit the authenticity of Eckermann's testimony by noting discrepancies between some of the dates of Eckermann's arrangement of his story as though it had been written-up in a diary, and other

[57] See my Eckermann article in *P.E.G.S.* The attack which first smeared Eckermann's reputation was by J. Petersen in *Die Entstehung der Eckermann'schen Gespräche und ihre Glaubwürdigkeit* (Berlin 1924).

sources of factual information about Goethe's life at this last stage. More radical critics joined in the hunt because they considered that the portrait Eckermann gave of his hero lacked warts or other signs of authenticity. Both these attacks have been proved unfounded: Eckermann's dates are indeed often out of accord with those in other sources, but it has in the meantime been shown that even the dates dictated into his own diary by the poet were inaccurate, and that some of the 'facts' to be found there were distorted by the inaccuracy of his secretaries; and on the other front, behind the apparent limpidity of Eckermann's 'Victorian' prose it can be seen that the Hamburg pedlar's son was well aware of some of the tensions of Goethe's life and did his best to bring them into his picture – but with a discretion which has become increasingly unfashionable since 1919.

Even if it were proved that Eckermann's picture of Goethe was more than somewhat fictional, his book would remain a remarkable testimony to the literary precepts of the great poet and the effects they could produce on a young man who might almost be called an autodidact, one of those '*Naturdichter*' in whom Goethe took an interest which foreshadowed the contemporary interest in primitive painters and other 'naturals'.[58] The story of the *Conversations* indeed illuminates Goethe's last decade in every respect. Their inception would seem to have been Goethe's interest in Napoleon and Byron; after the death of these heroes of the Romantic movement there was a striking output of journalistic literature about every corner of their lives, and notably about Napoleon's last years on St Helena. Parallel with this was the appearance of Medwin's collection of conversations with Byron. It could well be that Goethe had felt that he too ought to prepare to provide posterity with first-hand evidence of his last years: there was even an intimation of the literary immortality which was to come when J. D. Falk published some rather inferior conversations with the master in 1824. Goethe, moreover, could hardly have been unaware of the busy scribbling about himself which was going on in the studies of his old friends,

[58] U. Wertheim, essay on Goethe and 'Naturdichter' in *Goethe-Studien* (Berlin 1968).

the librarian Riemer and Weimar's Lord Chancellor, Müller, both ambitious men of letters.

Hence there can be no doubt that the old man was more than a little pleased when he discovered that his new helper had been writing up the conversations which they had been having about the editorial work which he had been given to do. Amongst these jobs (it will be recalled that they concerned preparations for the *Ausgabe letzter Hand*) Goethe gave Eckermann the copies of Merck's early 'little magazine' and told him to sort out from them his (anonymous) reviews. This was a stiff test of Eckermann's capacity to distinguish Goethe's style and he passed it with flying colours; in the course of this work, however, there were often occasions on which conversation turned to the subject-matter of the reviews. It was these which Eckermann wrote up in the first pages of his Weimar chronicle. It was to become the way in which he worked all through the first (and original) two books of his opus: the third book may well offer points on which Eckermann can be criticized, since it was written – in response to repeated requests from admirers ranging from former friends of Goethe to members of the general public – a decade and a half later, and on the basis of all kinds of material scratched together to fill out the author's own memory; for the young man, in his whole-hearted fashion, had completely exhausted his material in the original work.

Goethe's motives in encouraging his helper's note-taking were interesting. Vanity was there, of course; but it is incontrovertible that there was also a desire to overcome the censorship of expression which his position forced him to impose on himself with regard to many contemporary political and social issues. These come strongly to the fore in the pages of Eckermann's record; we have a fascinating picture of one of Europe's intellectual pillars waiting with almost bated breath for his daily consignment of French liberal journals. Only unbalanced political partisans could attack Goethe as a tool of reaction, as German radicals have attacked him, from the days of the 'Young Germans' (the 1820s, 1830s and 1840s) through the Expressionist storms of the First World War to the 'angry young men' of the 1960s.[59]

[59] W. Leppmann, *The German Image of Goethe* (Oxford 1961).

In addition to his reasoned, liberal survey of contemporary socio-political problems, Goethe was outspoken with his disciple in criticizing current literary trends. It could well be that it was this mocking characterization of the inept posings of the later Romantic writers which annoyed them to the point where they chose to belittle the author simply because he *was* a successful writer: one can cite similar attitudes amongst later revolutionaries in their own day towards Voltaire on the one hand and George Bernard Shaw and J. B. Priestley on the other. From the standpoint of European literature Goethe's work overall can be described as partaking of the 'Romantic syndrome': though Goethe's cast of mind was formed by the philosophical rationalism of his father's eighteenth-century training, he expressed his visions throughout in the vocabulary of Romanticism. It was for this reason that he was on such friendly terms, in both Life and Literature, with Byron, Scott, Manzoni, Mickiewicz and contemporary Romantics in Russia and the United States (amongst his visitors were George Ticknor and A. W. Everett).

In the years of the poet's early manhood, of course, our modern categorization of literary periods, by which we think of an Age of Reason followed (and attacked) by a Romantic movement, did not exist. Goethe and Schiller looked on contemporary literature simply as good or bad writing: they had the dramas of the Schlegel brothers produced on the Weimar stage under their aegis; they printed the early poems of Novalis and Hölderlin without second thoughts; if Goethe objected to the work of Heinrich von Kleist it was simply because he was as worried by Kleist's twisted psychology as many of his readers are still. It was only in the second decade of the nineteenth century that there began to arise a new generation of Romantic writers for whom Romanticism was more than a mere literary style. For these frustrated revolutionaries, growing up in the very deep shadows cast by the fame of such great writers as Goethe, their Romantic theories – interlocking with their ideological prejudices – began to imply more than a simple revision of attitudes to the craft of literature. It was their work which finally led Goethe to his damning criticism, made to Eckermann, in which he called Romantic literature 'unhealthy' compared with the 'healthiness' of Classical literature. This was not, moreover, simply a clever generalization or a 'terrible simplification' : it was documented by withering analyses of the weakness of the literary work of Platen, Börne, Werner and the so-called Swabian 'school' (Uhland, Müller, etc.).

Goethe did stand up to these new writers in his periodical journalism, but largely by omitting from consideration those works which seemed to him to be redolent of decay rather than health. For a professional writer of his standing it would have been as undignified as it would have been pointless for him to enter into polemics with younger writers. This was one reason why he chose to hide his really damaging criticisms in Eckermann's pages so that they should not be published until after his death. It was, one could say, to some extent a cowardly action, putting the onus for the unpopularity which would ensue on to poor Eckermann. With his lifelong faith in the destiny of great men (in Eckermann's pages this belief is often discussed in the form of Goethe's analysis of the magnetic powers of the man endowed with 'demonism' – we would say charisma), the poet allowed himself this moral luxury. He may be condemned for this – it is perhaps the weakest point in his character; yet there are few writers who may properly throw stones at him for lack of courage in his social life.

Indeed the views, when published, did not cause the general unpopularity which might have been anticipated. Had they been published ten years before Goethe's death in 1832 they would indeed have caused uproar. In the 1830s they were accepted, even by some of those criticized, though they might be regarded by the general reading public as the harmless soothsayings of a now dead Great Man, to be read and forgotten. Heinrich Laube, one of the more perceptive of the 'Young Germans', continued his patronage of Eckermann and was one of the most insistent among those who incited him to produce material for a third volume of reminiscences of Goethe's final years. Carlyle in England remained a staunch advocate of the great German poet. The Prussian equivalent of de Tocqueville, Varnhagen von Ense (in whose Berlin *salon* his wife, the celebrated Rahel Levin, had collected the last of the German Romantic coteries), followed the production of the *Conversations* with rapt interest and to all intents and purposes took over from Goethe as Eckermann's mentor and protector.

From Eckermann's description the course of Goethe's last decade becomes limpidly clear and we see what the radical Munich critic of the 1920s, Josef Hofmiller, savagely criticized, the guests thronging the marble-lined staircases and carrying on their conversations round the rococo chairs and settees.[60] Amongst the more revealing pictures immortalized in Eckermann's even prose are the many sessions in Goethe's print-room: in his early years in Weimar the young scholar was quite deliberately trained in art appreciation by his master, who constantly faced him with new etchings, engravings and other reproductions from his vast collection. This highlights a major facet of artistic appreciation in general in the Goethe period: it was long before the invention of colour photography, and it was indeed some time before the invention of photography brought the great European works of art within the view of those who could not travel to see them *in situ*. Goethe had had to build up for himself a satisfactory collection of reproductions of those works of art which were crucial for the vision of aestheticians in the mid-eighteenth century, like the central Laocoön group in the Vatican Museum which played such a key part in Winckelmann's and Lessing's view of Classical Antiquity and its art. He sometimes travelled a long way simply in order to visit collections which contained quite inferior plaster reproductions of antique statuary.

This had led Goethe to follow in the parental tradition and add to his father's collection of coins and busts a vast collection of engraved reproductions. He seems to have spent much time all through his life contemplating and discussing these, especially with his old friend the Swiss artist Heinrich Meyer, whom he attracted to Weimar as head of the art school. During Eckermann's apprenticeship Meyer would often be present as an active participant in the lesson, when Goethe would carefully extract

[60] J. Hofmiller, *Versuche* (Munich 1909). An interesting contribution which does not deliver as much as it promises is N. Fuerst, *The Victorian Age in German Literature* (Dobson 1965). There is more on the subject to be gained from J. P. Stern, *Re-interpretations* (Thames & Hudson 1964).

from its portfolio an engraving after Claude Lorrain or some Dutch master and teach the young man the elements of Classical form from a discussion of the images. This fondness for the visual arts continues throughout Eckermann's narrative, coming very noticeably to the surface, for example, much later, in his account of the discussion of Delacroix's designs for his illustrations to *Faust* when these were sent to the poet.

One of the most entertaining facets of Goethe's household routine at the end of his life is the poet's absorption in his collections. One result of the Renaissance cult of the virtuoso, the 'man of all the talents', had been the growth of collecting as an art; after the Renaissance, and especially in the early nineteenth century, increasing numbers of entrepreneurs earned their daily bread purveying collections to the cultured and the wealthy. Goethe participated to the full in this fashion; in addition to his prints and his casts he collected geological specimens, in particular, most of which he obtained himself on various expeditions. These had begun in the Thuringian hills, where he learnt his skill during visits of inspection as Commissioner of Mines, and he widened his field of operations to areas as rich in varied specimens as the Harz, which he visited no fewer than four times, and the Erzgebirge in Bohemia, where he spent so many of his holidays and where he was on very friendly terms with two great experts, the administrator Gruner and the noted geologist Graf von Sternberg. Goethe had the reputation of warming more readily to visitors who presented him with new material for his collections and was also not free of the collector's failing of hanging on to specimens left with him for inspection by incautious friends and acquaintances! He was entertained too by some of the tokens of respect given him by visitors; one of Eckermann's 'set pieces' in his third book pictures an afternoon in the garden of one of the master's residences where master and disciple shoot with a Bashkir cross-bow, presented to the poet by Russian officers who had called on him during the Napoleonic occupation of Germany by the Tsarist forces.

Another side of the old man's life is represented by Eckermann's descriptions of the poet's unaffected love for his three grandchildren, the daughter and sons of August and Ottilie. If one takes these scenes at their face value one may, like Hofmiller, dismiss them as Biedermeier idylls; viewing them against the background of the old man's turbulent domestic life in the preceding two decades one realizes that Eckermann is going out of his way to present a Goethe who had at last reached the calm seas of genuine resignation. Indeed, the picture is not always as idyllic as it might appear to be. When, for instance, the calm tenor of Eckermann's existence was shattered by Goethe's using him as a companion for his son's Italian journey – a journey which did not bring the young and impecunious autodidact the rich enjoyment it had brought the gay ex-minister of the Weimar court – the holiday was brought to a tragic conclusion by August's sudden death from a fever in Genoa. This was a tragedy for the old man – and Eckermann has a number of similarly unpleasant experiences to report, such as Goethe's mortal sorrow (expressed with great dignity) at the final illness and death of his old friend Duke Karl August.

What, finally, Eckermann showed only to his great defender, the radical professor who refuted his detractor of 1923, were the tensions that sprang up between himself and the poet from time to time, such as the occasion when after five years of faithful but inadequately rewarded service the young man's fiancée insisted that he should demand from his master a payment substantial enough to enable them to get married. Goethe's preoccupation with economizing may be explained partly by the generally low standard of living of the Weimar court and the royal master's comparative meanness; but one can also see in it the poet's solid bourgeois background. Though in the Romantic period middle-class men of letters were forging to the front of intellectual life, their financial rewards were still uncertain, and patronage was still their most profitable goal. Goethe also suffered considerably from the chaotic publishing conditions of the time, but he was famous enough to confront the publishers and gain copyright protection from the German Bund – the first modern writer to win a battle of this kind. Eckermann, it may be added, was not so successful. Not only did Goethe underpay him: he also lost a lawsuit against one of the leading publishers of the day, unjustly, by modern standards.

Chapter 13

The Worried Decade and its Products

No description of the Goethe scene can, in theory, be complete without some investigation of the large quantity of lyrical poetry which for many is Goethe's main claim to undying fame. But it is always better to read and listen to poetry than to discuss it, or if, for scientific purposes, it has to be discussed, it must be discussed in great detail. This has been done by Emil Staiger in German and by Ronald Gray in English,[61] and it would simply expand this study unnecessarily to toy with the poetry in a dilettante fashion.

Suffice it to say that Goethe never lost his genius for putting down on paper those carefully chosen German words which encapsulate for all subsequent readers so many thoughts on so many subjects, and notably the seasons, the times of day, and the great and simple features of external Nature. Since so much lyrical poetry was triggered off in him by his 'repeated puberty', very many of his verses may be associated with the women whose beauty or whose minds captivated him at the time. But all kinds of other thoughts could stimulate him to poetic productivity: thus there is a charming series of miniature poems which he was inspired to write quite late in life by a reading of translations from the Chinese, and another magnificent poem was inspired by his being shown the skull of his friend and collaborator, Schiller. Many other great lines were inspired by momentary occurrences

[61] E. Staiger, *Goethe*, 3 vols (Bern 1952–). For Gray's 'critical introduction' see 37. Some of the soundest judgements by a German critic are found in H. A. Korff, *Geist der Goethezeit*, 4 vols (Leipzig 1923–).

or by fluctuations in his state of mind, for example, the solemn but beautiful poems written on a retreat in the ducal castle of Dornburg in his old age, which they lament, but without disheartening the reader.

Mention may also be made of many occasional writings, on a bewildering variety of topics. A fascinating aspect of any poet's production are the notebooks in which he records ideas as they occur to him. In this respect Goethe's instinct for methodically assembling his files has made him one of the best-documented writers of all time. Many volumes of the posthumous works are devoted to collections of writings with such titles as 'Maxims and Reflections', 'Views on Art, on Literature', etc. And, to complement this astonishing publishing of his whole *Weltanschauung*, his own deliberate encouragement of Eckermann to record his conversations incited many of his other friends and colleagues to record impressions of their intercourse with him. Thus there has come into being a vast stock of accounts of conversations with Goethe which were assembled into a kind of biographical concordance by Biedermann in 1909 and were being reassembled until his death by the late Ernst Grumach.[62] In this field, of course, Eckermann maintains his priority, but there are important collections of memoirs by other people, such as Riemer and Chancellor von Müller, in particular, all of which have been authenticated in this century by the most rigorous scholarship.

It would seem that Goethe's methodical collecting habit had deeper roots than a mere indulgence in self-documentation. Certainly the poet's own life was almost completely covered in the ways in which he wished it to be: he himself wrote one of the world's best autobiographies, covering the period of his life up to his departure for Weimar in 1775, the four-volume *Dichtung und Wahrheit*, whose separate books appeared in 1811, 1812, 1814 and 1831 respectively. There were many personal reasons why he was unwilling to give a similarly detailed treatment to the

[62] Biedermann, *Goethes Gespräche*, 5 vols (Berlin 1909–11). Reprinted many times since, these are now in process of re-issue in new critical form by the Grumachs. Perhaps their best achievement so far is their revised edn of the conversations with Kanzler *v.* Müller (Weimar 1959). On their work see the *Nachwort* to *Goethe im Gespräch* (Fischer-Bücherei 1960).

first decade of his life in Weimar – respect for the feelings of Frau von Stein and Karl August were two of the most important reasons for this reticence. This period is accordingly less well documented than any subsequent one. But the poet himself saw the importance of assembling into one work of art his impressions of Italy, and the result was the magnificent *Italienische Reise*, which is based to a considerable extent on the letters sent by Goethe during his wanderings to Frau von Stein. After that the only experiences which received separate treatment were his military campaigns in the entourage of Karl August during the Wars of Intervention – two shorter works give life to these episodes of the 1790s. But the rest of his life was not left entirely undocumented. He tried to keep a kind of diary from the time he returned from Italy, although the undertaking did not become systematic until he took to retaining a permanent secretary to whom he could dictate what was passing through his mind. Even in this, however, he was not entirely systematic, and the attempted *catalogue raisonné* of his thoughts and undertakings, the *Annalen* and subsequent *Tag- und Jahreshefte*, were not the methodical record one might have expected, as they were sometimes ignored for weeks on end, and were often interrupted by travelling. There is none the less a remarkable record, in diaries, in autobiography, in maxims and in conversation, so much so that biographers never tire of distilling from it further portraits of the great man. It is interesting to reflect how much of this goes back to the poet's own decision to write *Dichtung und Wahrheit*, which is itself so much more than a simple autobiography.

In 1801 Goethe suffered a severe bronchial illness which almost carried him off. By contemporary standards he was no longer a young man, and he was seized by fear of sudden death. This made him begin to assemble the records of his early life. An introspective undertaking of this kind was also encouraged by the general intellectual gloom of the first decade of the nineteenth century. Certainly there were moments of elevation, such as the Erfurt meeting with Napoleon, but Goethe's life in this period was intellectually unhappy, interwoven as it was by the growing realization of the fundamental unsuitability of his alliance with Christiane, which simple decency compelled him to make into a legal marriage in 1806. Despite this the decade was also marked by the passionate affair with Silvie von Ziegesar. In addition there was the strong passing attraction ('more acute than was sensible', said Goethe himself) for the pretty young foster-daughter of the Jena publisher, Fromann, Minna Herzlieb.

Out of this frustrated decade Goethe emerged to attempt to write the story of his life. In many ways it was also the story of his heart; but the astonishing thing about the autobiography is the way in which the scientist Goethe turned the life-story into a research project, not simply into the emergence of a poet but into the whole epoch which influenced him. So thorough-going was Goethe's sounding of the state of German literature in his early days that his method of working on the study may be said to have laid the foundations for German nineteenth-century literary historiography.[63] Into this study too there flowed that uncovering of psychological motivation which, as noted in an earlier chapter, was so fruitful for the emergence of the modern psychological novel. Perhaps because of this, *Dichtung und Wahrheit* is not the objective photograph of a childhood and adolescence which is demanded by a strictly scientific biography. It is a work of art and as such takes its place amongst the creative writings of the poet.

There are many features about the 'autobiography' which are of interest from this standpoint. Mention has been made before of the way in which our appreciation of Friederike has been completely conditioned by the way the poet presented his first meeting with her and their subsequent relationship in the style of *The Vicar of Wakefield*, which he was engaged in studying at the time. In fact we have no first-hand evidence about Friederike, and only some very dubious contemporary likenesses. Similarly Goethe writes into the description of his earlier life in Frankfurt a romantic episode with a music-master's daughter called Gretchen, which has given critics ever since material for all kinds of exegeses. The point is that this was precisely what Goethe intended: the original title of the work was *Wahrheit und Dichtung*, and the word order was only changed in the interests

[63] Braemer, *Goethes Prometheus. . . .* See first and last sections.

of euphony. But the original title suggests, more clearly than the second, that the poet thought of the work from the start merely as a description of the truth in so far as it *helped explain the poetry*. In this Goethe has not only set an example for subsequent autobiographers in Germany; he influenced the whole style of nineteenth-century German literary criticism, especially of his own work. When Wilhelm Scherer and Franz Mehring tried to break with the tradition at the century's end, they still exercised their positivistic skills on the details provided by Goethe. The scholars of the period immediately preceding and following the First World War sometimes got away from the tradition, simply because they were men of the twentieth century and were familiar with foreign as well as German culture: being pupils of the *art nouveau* poet Stefan George they had quite different preoccupations. But it was not really until the most recent period, when English and American 'new critical' ideas wafted into Germany, that new looks have been taken at Goethe's biography in any light except that in which he presented it in *Dichtung und Wahrheit*.[64]

At the same time the literary merits of the autobiography should not be overlooked. Like Schiller's historiography in his *Dreissigjähriger Krieg*, Goethe's literary criticism seduces through its elegant style. Goethe was always a quite irresistible correspondent: one does not need to develop any wizardry with stylistics to learn to appreciate the tripping and romping Goethe prose. Even where it is scientific or administrative it has almost the ring of hexameters; no matter what the context, the poet streaks ahead putting together all manner of new words to express what is in his mind. In his verse this is most enjoyable; in his prose it sometimes makes his meaning obscure, as in the famous phrase in which he called *Faust 'inkommensurabel'*. We can easily under-

[64] Braemer, op. cit., reviews briefly many of the standard works, with summary justice according to her Marxist standpoint. The standard biographies by Scherer, Kuno Fischer, etc. down to Emil Ludwig and Friedenthal will be found in most libraries. Of more recent monographs in German I would single out Günter Müller, R. Buchwald and Grete Schaeder, and special studies by Fritz Strich, M. Mommsen, Max Kommerell and Hans S. Reiss (the last originally in English).

stand what the meaning ought to be from the word's semantic history, but we are not justified in accepting any special meaning in Goethe's particular collocation until we know much more about Goethe's prose habits with regard to such words: this is an area where in the past some dreadful solecisms have been committed. It is made all the more dangerous an area because from an early period Goethe used many foreign words: at first they were the modish French and Italian words of the rococo; later they extended to a good many English words and also technical designations borrowed from his massive reading of French and English scientists and economists.[65]

It is not necessary to give any elucidation of the autobiography beyond saying that the four books cover Goethe's life from his birth to the time he left Frankfurt for Weimar. Where it is necessary to narrate, the poet does so; but side by side with narrative *cum* studio-portraits, as one may call them, of the important men and women in his life, more self-consciously psychological and analytical than any yet attempted in German autobiography. The studio-portraits of the autobiography seem to be of the same order of penetration as the great series of actual portraits of his circle done during Goethe's lifetime by the Austrian painter Anton Graff or the drawings of his friends done in his last years by the Bavarian J. J. Schmeller. In each case these painters (like their English contemporaries Lawrence and Ramsay) raise portraiture from being simply a decorative art to being a branch of psychology. So it is with the pen-portraits of *Dichtung und Wahrheit*.

It was perhaps in the sophistication which he gave to German prose that Goethe left behind his most enduring monument in German literature. No doubt posterity has been terribly impressed by *Faust*, but the language of *Faust*, like the language of a great deal of Goethe's later work, is often orotund to the point where one thinks of one word – 'Victorian'. A brief example of this may be seen in the famous 'Novelle', which Francis Bennett held to be the actual source of the development in Germany of the genre

[65] The Deutsche Akademie der Wissenschaften has been producing ever since 1945 a special Goethe Dictionary. So vast is the enterprise that so far only five fascicles have appeared.

of that name. Goethe was in this prose gobbet competing with the later Romantic writers, whose 'unhealthy' imaginations (as Goethe called them) revelled only in fairy-tale and religious subjects. The unreal subject-matter of the 'Novelle' clearly falls into this category: a lion escapes from a travelling circus in what looks like a medieval time-scape, gives considerable palpitations to the court and one or two of its members especially, but is finally brought back to captivity by the tamer's little son who pipes to it and reduces it to a degree of docility which is described with loathsome smugness. But both scenically and stylistically one is also reminded of those German 'Nazarene' painters, the forerunners of our Pre-Raphaelite Brotherhood, whom the poet so hated but whom he has here almost plagiarized.[66]

This point is mentioned here because it is from the stylistic angle that the gravest criticisms may be levelled against two of the major works of the poet's last great period, *Die Wahlverwandtschaften* (1808), and the continuation of *Wilhelm Meister*, the *Wanderjahre* (published first in 1821 but not put out in Goethe's own final version until the second actual, but first full, edition in the *Ausgabe letzter Hand* of 1828). The two works are here brought together in a final homage to the poet because they have much in common in their content and in their reflection of Goethe's personality. Both novels suffer from their 'Victorian' style but contain material which is, from the standpoint of the nineteenth century, astonishing and almost revolutionary. It is only necessary to read the great expositors of the nineteenth century – Hermann Grimm, Düntzer and Bielschowsky in German, Carlyle, Lewes and Robertson in English[67] – to see how little understanding these contemporaries or near-contemporaries

[66] The Nazarenes have recently been described by H. S. Andrews. Otherwise they are to be read up only in the histories of German 19th-century art, e.g. W. Neuss, *Das Wesen der Nazarener-Kunst* (Augsburg n.d. *c.* 1926).

[67] All these names will be found in the catalogues of big libraries, though the warning must be issued that much of the interpretation will no longer hold water, from contemporary standpoints, and the language is needlessly mandarin and difficult. One of the most fascinating sides of Anglo-German relations, Carlyle's view of Goethe, has yet to be satisfactorily explored (Bruford touched on it in a Goethe Society address).

of the great man had of what was really in his mind. They accepted the moral and sociological criteria of the nineteenth-century consensus as though they had been written on Mosaic tablets; Goethe accepted nothing, but thought everything through from first principles.

At the same time both novels are firmly rooted in the poet's life. Like H. J. Geerdts,[68] one may consider that Wolff tends to overestimate the part played in Goethe's life by Silvie von Ziegesar; yet one must still consider that it was this combination of an unhappy married life with an impossible love for a truly innocent but none the less healthily sensuous young girl which finally persuaded Goethe that there was small room in life for real happiness, but that consolation could only come from resignation. This is the ultimate moral of *Wahlverwandtschaften*, and the sub-title of the *Wanderjahre* is *Die Entsagenden*. Since, as we shall see, Goethe certainly did not mean this in the sociological and economic sense, we must accept that he meant it to signify the relationships between men and women, which becomes clear from the many individual stories included in the work. And it is noteworthy that most of these individual narratives, in so far as they form self-contained novella-type entities, were written between 1807 and 1810; so strongly did Goethe think of them as independent units that he made considerable changes in their place in the narrative between the first *Wanderjahre* of 1821 and the final edition. This final edition of 1828 is itself an extraordinary work: Goethe had allocated to it three volumes of the *Ausgabe letzter Hand*, but when the manuscript finally went to the printer it was obvious that the second and third books would be much thinner than the norm. Not a whit worried, and, as will be seen, perfectly happy to depart from what was to become the nineteenth century's dogma of the '*roman bien fait*', the octogenarian simply thrust into Eckermann's hands some fat files of aphorisms and told him to choose from these sufficient to produce volumes of the required circumference. These two collections, he suggested, could be put in or removed at will, and in

[68] H. J. Geerdts, *Goethes Roman 'Die Wahlverwandtschaften'* (Berlin 1966) is an interesting Marxist study.

later editions they have usually been proffered separately: they form the two collections, *Betrachtungen im Sinne der Wanderer*, and *Aus Makariens Archiv*.

Die Wahlverwandtschaften, as it has been analysed by H. M. Wolff,[69] consists of one novel into which at a slightly later date was inserted a large elaboration which turned it into a three-volume work. Goethe was, according to the evidence of his diaries, anything but satisfied with the first version and soon began to think about recasting it. Work may even have begun in 1808; the decisive steps were certainly taken, according to the diaries, in May 1809, when a completely new section was finally drafted which, when inserted, together with one or two minor additions, between the end of the first original book of the manuscript and the denouement, gave the book its final shape. This reasoning of Wolff's is accepted by and large by Geerdts and makes sense of many things which in this final version are unclear. It is obvious, from any study of Barnes's closely reasoned analysis of the novel, that the existing story is full of *non sequiturs*, both in the plot and, above all, in the development of the characters. However much one may doubt, with Geerdts, the important role allotted to Silvie by Wolff, there is every reason to accept the latter's final judgement as to the motives behind the alterations the novelist made to his original story.

As is well known, the title of Goethe's novel refers to the fact that in certain chemical processes the addition of one compound to another will cause the constituents of the first compound to be dissolved and combine with the constituents of the second, so that in the end we have, instead of the two compounds AB and XY, the two compounds AY and BX. Goethe takes this chemical finding as an objective correlative for what happens to the marriage of his protagonists, Eduard and Charlotte. It is not a remarkable story compared with many novels of earlier periods. What was new was the main character's decision to solve definitively the dreadful problem posed by his change of affection, to end his first marriage in divorce. Had this idea been carried to its logical conclusion, we should indeed have had a

[69] See too Wolff and Barnes, op. cit. (nn. 55 and 56).

novel which, by the standards of the time, was highly immoral. Eduard behaves in a way which Wolff characterizes as 'brutal'; he does not seem to be a very edifying person. This too might not have worried Goethe, who had himself faced a very similar problem in the years leading up to 1808. But he did *not* cut his own Gordian knot in the way which he recommended to his hero; indeed he made it tighter by actually marrying Christiane in 1806, despite his fitful yearnings for the virginal Silvie. So he could not remain entirely happy with the wishful thinking in which he had indulged in the novel. Therefore he toyed with new plot elements until he finally lighted on a solution which changed the novel considerably. At the height of the crisis Eduard had suggested a period of cooling off, which Goethe motivated by sending him off to a recently erupted war. In this interim period Goethe now changed the plot considerably. He invented a fourth character, a retired military man, who comes to stay in the house. Charlotte feels herself more and more drawn to him – which gives her a share in the general guilt. This is underlined when the child who is born to Eduard and Charlotte (as the result of a temporary emotional *rapprochement*) proves to have the physical lineaments of the captain and Ottilie (whose persons had filled the minds of the two chief protagonists even in their physical union). To crown everything, however, Ottilie, who has had her mind gradually changed by living in Charlotte's house during Eduard's absence, devotes herself to nursing the child but allows it, in a moment of love-crazed distraction, to drown. This tragic event so works on her that she goes into a decline and dies, thus removing the catalyst from the chemicals.

The final version of this novel is an impressive achievement, even allowing for the fact that the strangely loaded style makes it unusually difficult to read. The most unusual aspect of it is precisely the fact that its new morality separates it almost entirely from the earlier works of the poet. Hard experience taught the poet an attitude to sex which only became widely accepted in the first third of this century, and which is still being denied by many people brought up within strictly Christian guidelines. That continence and marital fidelity are now becoming rarer phenomena merely confirms last-ditch defenders of the old churches in their view that this neglect is the fundamental source of trouble in modern life.

Goethe's hard experience was his own life with Christiane in Weimar, and his sudden urge, in the years after his illness, to live again and possibly even to link his own fate with some new mate chosen this time with the insight which experience gives an adult. If Fairley's reading of the poet's belated sexual development is accepted, in fact, one could call the liaison with Christiane the kind of blind choice which young men are all too apt to make.[70] The events of Goethe's seventh decade thus resemble the kind of restlessness which comes over many married men after their first ten years of marriage. To have made this into literature was ruthlessly honest, even though undoubtedly unwise.

This was doubtless why the poet wished to make the novel much more *nuancé* than it seemed to be in the first version. Moreover, he had not been at all certain that his first version corresponded to any truth, either aesthetic or psychological. He himself, far from modelling his conduct on Eduard's, had done something completely quixotic in actually marrying the woman who caused him so much trouble with her growing coarseness and her constantly increasing indulgence in alcohol and vulgar flirtations. But leaving this aspect entirely aside, Goethe could not be sure in his own mind that there was not more to be said for resignation; in Freudian terms he realized the creative value of repression. How fruitful this was to become can be seen in the *Wanderjahre*.

[70] Fairley, *A Study of Goethe*.

Chapter 14

The Utopian Perfection

The last decade of Goethe's life is wonderfully documented in the pages of Eckermann's *Gespräche mit Goethe*. The discussion which this book has caused in the last half-century has rested on the challenge to its authenticity by modern critics of Goethe. In the nineteenth century it was accepted as the authentic record, and some of its faults – Eckermann's timidity often causes him to sound much more conformist than either he or Goethe actually was – gave ammunition to the detractors of the great man. Amongst these 'faults', according to some of the modern critics, is the fact that Eckermann did not simply report the conversations of his master; he often gave them a background, so that we actually seem to be living at Goethe's side, like his chronicler. In this respect Eckermann may be said to be much more of a creative writer than Boswell, with whom he has often been compared. We visit the Goethe household with Eckermann, we take tea on the lawn or watch the poet drawing etchings from his portfolios.

Amid the daily routine of business which is minutely described there is hardly anything which is of more moment than the sight of Goethe opening his mail and commenting on what has just arrived. It was an obvious ploy for a chronicler of *obiter dicta*, but it is also psychologically very feasible. Amongst the things in his mail to which it would thus appear that the old man most looked forward was the arrival of the French journals. These were almost wholly the great liberal journals of the 1820s, and included, in particular, *Le Globe*, one of the foremost mouthpieces of that French radicalism which still burned fiercely despite the European movement of Restoration following the Congress of Vienna.

It is in comment on items from these papers that we often hear of Goethe's continued and forward-looking interest in such matters as the Suez Canal, political movements in Ireland and America, and indeed many issues which bring the old man close to us today.

From Goethe's library and the names of the books he read, which he noted down in his diaries, we realize how very up to date he kept himself in his interests, notably in the sphere of economics. It was a great period for the development of modern social theory, and it is with no little astonishment and growing enthusiasm that we read of the old man's intense interest in and approval of the works of radical thinkers from Bentham and Robert Owen to Saint-Simon, Fourier and Sismondi. Ursula Wertheim's detailed study of the *Westöstlicher Divan*[71] shows us that such reading was accompanied by creative work inspired by his deep sympathy for the radical ideas which were in the air. Perhaps the most striking example of this is in the last book of the *Wanderjahre*, one of the very last of the poet's major writings, for it was only added in 1828 and 1829, just before the final version was given to the printer for the *Ausgabe letzter Hand*.

Wilhelm Meister, like *Faust*, accompanied Goethe all through his life. The original version of 1782–6 (sketched, if Wolff is right, in 1772–3) breathes the spirit of Sturm und Drang, though in an aesthetic embodiment. Wilhelm Meister, a young man of impeccable bourgeois background (like Goethe), is drawn increasingly towards the theatre, where he falls deeply in love with a young actress. Heart-broken by her frivolity, he goes off and joins a strolling troupe with which he makes a brilliant acting debut; he is taken up by a wealthy count, in whose castle he helps the troupe to perform, and is finally drawn into a leading professional troupe in a big capital city. There is little overt political criticism of contemporary Germany in all this, though there are shrewd *aperçus* of social behaviour, notably in the descriptions of life at the count's court.

In 1795–6 Goethe reworked this version and achieved the final version, called *Wilhelm Meisters Lehrjahre*. The planless revolt

[71] Wertheim, *Von Tasso bis Hafis*, goes sympathetically into this.

against bourgeois society of the early version was now turned into a gradual apprenticeship to real life. Meister's early turning away from business to the theatre was retained, but compressed, and the spotlight fell on the new chapters; it now appeared that the early odyssey had not been as aimless as it seemed but was guided by a secret society, a kind of masonic lodge, which was training the young hothead and preparing him for a great career of what today would be called social service. The members of the Society of the Tower are the kind of enlightened aristocrats whose efforts laid the foundations for the Revolution in France. Though Goethe only occasionally spells out the *philosophe* ideas of the Society in explicit terms the spirit of the Society permeates all the final chapters.

The ending of the *Lehrjahre* undoubtedly left the poet dissatisfied. He not only disapproved of the loose ends which he had left; he felt that he had not done full justice to the ideas of the *philosophes*, though, as many of his liberal-minded contemporaries found, it was difficult in the turbulent days of the Revolutionary wars to put them into any firm shape. It took him, in fact, all of thirty years to clear his mind on this score. When he did take up the story again in the unhappy years which saw the production of *Die Wahlverwandtschaften*, what emerged were various plans for a continuation; half a dozen stories were ultimately linked, some organically, with the final version, to which, following the German artisan custom (the successful *Lehrling* used to set out on a period of *Wanderjahre*), he gave its appropriate name.

The plan for the *Wanderjahre* first finds mention in the diaries in 1796 but it was not until 1810 that he began to write any of the final chapters. These were then re-cast, together with the stories of 1807–10, to form the version which was printed in one volume in 1821. This 'final' version was only a step on the way, however. It did not contain the Utopian chapters dealing with economics of the last version of 1828–9. But it did contain the essentials of the story, to which the sub-title *Die Entsagenden* (The Renouncers) was to be given. Above all other renunciations is that made by Wilhelm, who is not allowed to settle down in wedded bliss with his Natalie but is sent out with his illegitimate child by the young actress of the *Theatralische Sendung*, to gain further experience of the world. He may not stay longer than three days in any one place and is obviously being led along a carefully planned path of maturation. He learns to appreciate the value of hard work (especially of skilled artisan labour, which Goethe places – as did many of the Utopians of the day – in the forefront of social development) and, like all the other members of the Society, devotes himself to a particular skill. He becomes a surgeon, this also being taken as a form of skilled artisan work, and ultimately, in a highly symbolical episode, is able to use his skill to save his own son's life.

The education of Wilhelm's son, Felix, adds one more thread to the strands of the complicated plot. It leads Wilhelm to a special '*pädagogische Provinz*', a whole county which is devoted to the encouragement of a Utopian form of education. This is one of the most forward-looking parts of the whole novel; it is interesting, moreover, because of the great influence it has had on German education. In the first place, it led to the development by the followers of Rudolf Steiner (who began as editor of Goethe's scientific works for the great Weimar Sophien-Ausgabe) of the Waldorf-Schulen, 'progressive' schools with an impressive record of achievement which form the bulk of the private sector of modern German education. But the ambience of the *Wanderjahre* has also been that of almost all the great educational movements of the last hundred years in Germany; it was in the mind of Froebel; it inspired the Expressionist works on education by Wedekind, Döblin and Hermann Hesse; and it was part of the thought of creative German pedagogues and educational innovators like Kerschensteiner, Wyneken, Reichwein and Grimme.[72] To the impetus of *Wilhelm Meister* and, above all, the guiding idea of this last part, may well be attached the unfolding of the idea of the Wandervögel, the great movement of boys' and girls'

[72] A penetrating review of this line in German education is in Samuel and R. H. Thomas, *Education and Society in Modern Germany* (London 1949). There have been many studies on this and germane topics in the political field in German, notably from and about the 20th-century Youth Movement. Some of the flavour is conveyed by W. Laqueur in *Young Germany* (London 1962).

clubs which has been one of the most positive features of German social life in the last half-century.

The story-line of the novel is difficult to follow, because, in this so-called continuation, Goethe threw overboard many of the conventions which were beginning to be considered as essential for the novel. Just as in *Die natürliche Tochter* and other dramatic fragments of his later period, not to mention the second part of *Faust*, Goethe discarded normal elements of the nineteenth-century theatre, so here he treated the form of the traditional novel with a cavalier disregard which horrified orthodox critics until our contemporary authors suddenly lighted on the same idea and began to write novels which also had no obvious beginning, middle and end. Goethe did carry on many of the threads of the *Lehrjahre* but he treated them very arbitrarily. Moreover his developing outlook changed many of them radically. As Bielschowsky[73] has noted, this applies particularly to the character of the benign Oheim, whose castle forms the seat of the Tower Society at the end of the *Lehrjahre*. In the original novel the Oheim was indeed a paragon, but his ideal of perfection was that of the eighteenth century: it was a perfection which was essentially aristocratic and individualistic. His 'perfect man' was largely a continuation of Castiglione's 'courtier' and Shaftesbury's 'virtuoso', and was expressed by Goethe and Schiller themselves in their idea of the '*schöne Seele*'.

In the *Wanderjahre* the Oheim changes. For one thing he is now given a very concrete background. He is an American, descended from one of those religious pioneers who emigrated with William Penn. He has vast possessions in the New World but has been so impressed by the culture of the Old that he has settled back here in an attempt to combine the advantages of the two areas. Eckermann shows us how deeply Goethe was impressed by the possibilities of the New World. Like millions of Germans who exchanged the German 'Misere' (as Marx called it) for 'pastures new' in the nineteenth century, Goethe saw that there might be everything to be said for giving up the unequal struggle and attempting to make a clean start in an area which

[73] One of the classical biographies: A. Bielschowsky, *Goethe*, 2 vols (Munich 1896–1903).

still seemed open to Utopian planning. Hence the Oheim runs his large German estates on Utopian lines and inspires the whole of his widespread family with the ideals of work and social service, and particularly his nephew Lenardo, a new character. In the *Lehrjahre* the *'chevalier sans peur et sans reproche'* was Lothario (another nephew), but even he was stigmatized by individualistic sins more suitable to the eighteenth century than the nineteenth (it is he who broke the heart of Aurelie, the tragic sister of Wilhelm's entrepreneurial colleague Serlo). Now Goethe introduces a truly 'modern' figure who has not merely followed his uncle as a paternalistic manager of his family estates but is collecting a large company of first-rate artisans and farmers and preparing them to emigrate. He indeed consciously shuns paternalism and has educated his band of brothers in a form of democracy, so that he is simply *primus inter pares*, in spite of being their star and guide. His full development does not, in fact, come until the third book where, basing himself on the economic theories of the Western radicals, Goethe goes into considerable detail about the emigrants, their organization in Germany, and the province they colonize in America. In the third book, too, Wilhelm accompanies them. Like Carl Schurz (Abraham Lincoln's right-hand man) and so many energetic young men whose presence in Germany might have stiffened the puny resistance of German liberalism to autocracy, Wilhelm Meister and the Society of the Tower ultimately leave the shores of the Old World.[74]

By this time a great many of the tangled threads of the *Lehrjahre* have been sorted out – and many new ones added and re-sorted. The handful of short stories which were written during Goethe's worried decade were so carefully woven into the new plot that the cast of 'Der Mann von 50 Jahren', for example,

[74] There is a large literature in the U.S.A. on migration of Germans to the U.S.A. Very little of it, however, does justice to the theme of Utopianism struck here. One part of the migration went to Australia and I dealt with this aspect in 'The Germans in S. Australia', *Ger. Life and Letters*, Vol. IX (1956). The Utopianism is put in an even wider context in what might be called the definitive book on such religious migration: D. Pike, *Paradise of Dissent* (Melbourne 1968).

ultimately become characters in the novel and help to sort out the novel's climax. This development is all the more remarkable because the plot of the novella began as one of the 'great confessions' of the worried decade, being the story at first of a middle-aged man who discovers that his son's intended has fallen in love with him. The happy ending which the poet gave this imbroglio obviously worried him and it is not surprising to find that the story was written during the period in which the poet began work on *Die Wahlverwandtschaften*, which in some ways – but with what a difference! – deals with the same problem. A similar growth into the major plot happened to another of these stories, 'Das nußbraune Mädchen', whose heroine becomes an important linking factor in the quest on which Wilhelm is engaged; she emerges ultimately as the intended of Lenardo.

If there is one characteristic common to all these stories, and particularly to the endings given them in the *Wanderjahre*, it is that all end on the note of *Entsagung*. Perhaps the most strikingly symbolical piece is 'Die neue Melusine', the story (a typical fairy-tale motif) of the man who constantly fails to carry out the tasks set him by his blessed damozel; he eventually marries her despite the revelation that she is really a dwarf, and she metamorphoses him with the aid of a magic ring. But wearying of his miniaturized existence, he files through the ring, and loses his love and all his happiness. This is Goethe's final symbol for the artist and the idealist. There is much satisfaction, he says, to be had along the way by working hard in fellowship with people of like mind; but complete bliss (symbolized in most cases by the perfect sexual satisfaction of happily wedded status) is purely a magic dream.

Nevertheless *Wilhelm Meisters Wanderjahre* is the most impressive monument to the work of Goethe in his final period, more impressive in many ways than *Faust Part Two*, which was, as Goethe confessed, 'extorted' from him by the trusty Eckermann. To many, the end of the drama is a conventional apotheosis added as a pendant to the Prologue in Heaven, but without much real conviction. Despite the deliberately fragmentary form of the *Wanderjahre* Germany has, in this novel, a powerful message of the type which H. G. Wells was constantly trying to convey, but under the handicap of not being a poet. If a residue of idealism has survived amongst Germans throughout the ghastly history of their last century and a half it is not least because of these fires lit by their country's greatest poet.

Index

www.ingramcontent.com/pod-product-compliance
Lightning Source LLC
Chambersburg PA
CBHW070546100726
47907CB00004B/1289

* 9 7 8 1 0 3 2 8 2 0 6 1 3 *